Writing About
WORLD
LITERATURE

Writing About
WORLD
LITERATURE

KAREN M. GOCSIK

Dartmouth College

with contributions by

ROBERT KIRSCHEN

University of Nevada, Las Vegas

W. W. NORTON & COMPANY

New York • London

W. W. Norton & Company has been independent since its founding in 1923, when William Warder Norton and Mary D. Herter Norton first published lectures delivered at the People's Institute, the adult education division of New York City's Cooper Union. The firm soon expanded its program beyond the Institute, publishing books by celebrated academics from America and abroad. By midcentury, the two major pillars of Norton's publishing program—trade books and college texts—were firmly established. In the 1950s, the Norton family transferred control of the company to its employees, and today—with a staff of four hundred and a comparable number of trade, college, and professional titles published each year—W. W. Norton & Company stands as the largest and oldest publishing house owned wholly by its employees.

Editor: Peter Simon
Assistant editor: J. Conor Sullivan
Managing editor, College: Marian Johnson
Project editor: Kate Feighery
Copyeditor: Michele Lansing
Production manager: Benjamin Reynolds
Design director: Rubina Yeh
Series design: Chris Welch
Composition and project management: Westchester Book Group
Manufacturing: Courier—Westford, MA

Library of Congress Cataloging-in-Publication Data has been applied for.

ISBN: 978-0-393-91880-9

W. W. Norton & Company, Inc., 500 Fifth Avenue, New York, N.Y. 10110-0017
www.wwnorton.com
W. W. Norton & Company Ltd., Castle House, 75/76 Wells Street, London WIT 3QT

4   5   6   7   8   9   0

Brief Contents

Contents

Contents

Contents

Contents

Contents

1

What Is Academic Writing?

This short guide to writing about world literature provides information about the nature and process of academic writing in general, as well as information about the specific challenges involved in writing about world literature. Whether or not you've already taken a writing course, you should find guidance here that will help you complete whatever writing assignments you receive in your world literature class. The first topic we should tackle is the most general of all: What is academic writing?

Simply put, academic writing (sometimes called "scholarship") is writing done by scholars for other scholars—and that includes you. As a college student, you are engaged in activities that scholars have been engaged in for centuries: you will read about, think about, argue about, and write about great ideas. Of course being a scholar requires that you read, think, argue, and write in certain ways. You will need to make and support your claims according to the customary expectations of the academic community.

How do you determine what these expectations are? The literary theorist Kenneth Burke has famously described scholarship as an ongoing conversation, and this metaphor may be helpful. Imagine you have just arrived at a dinner party. The discussion (which in this case is about world literature) has already been going on for quite a while when you arrive. What do you do? Do you sit down and immediately voice your opinions? Or do you listen, try to gauge the lay of the land, determine what contribution you might make, and only then venture to make it?

The etiquette that you would employ at the dinner party is precisely the strategy that you should use when you write academic papers. In short, listen to what other scholars are saying. Familiarize yourself with the scholarly conversation before jumping in. Pay attention to both *what* is said and *how* it is said. A book like *The Norton Anthology of World Literature* is the perfect "dinner companion" for scholarship about world literature, getting you up to speed and filling you in on the conversation that preceded you. But you should make use of other resources, too. Your professor, for instance, is a living, breathing expert on what scholars of world literature care about. Books, journals, and even credible Internet sites also offer an opportunity to eavesdrop on the ongoing scholarly conversation about world literature. Once you understand the substance of that conversation, you can begin to construct informed arguments of your own.

Getting Started

CONSIDER WHAT YOU KNOW

When you sit down to write an academic paper, you'll first want to consider what you know about your topic. Different writing assignments require different degrees of knowledge. A short paper written in response to an episode from Murasaki Shikibu's *The Tale of Genji*, for example, may not require you to be familiar with the history of eleventh-century Japan.

However, if you're asked to write an academic paper on the novel, you'll want to know more. You'll want to have a sense of the basic outlines of medieval Japanese history and culture, as well as some knowledge of the author's biography. You'll want to familiarize yourself with the poetic tradition that preceded the novel so that you can understand the themes that were important to Murasaki and her contemporaries. Finally, if you're writing a research paper on this novel, you may be asked to be aware of different critical perspectives on *The Tale of Genji* so that you can place your argument within the ongoing critical conversation.

CONSIDER WHAT YOU THINK

The aim in thinking about your topic is to come up with fresh observations. After all, it's not enough to summarize in a paper what's obvious, what's already known and discussed. You must also add something of your own to the conversation.

Understand, however, that "adding something of your own" is not an invitation to allow your own personal associations, reactions, or experiences to dominate your paper. To create an informed argument, you must first recognize that your writing should be analytical rather than personal. In other words, your writing must show that your associations, reactions, and experiences of a work of literature have been framed in a critical, rather than a personal, way.

This is not to say that your personal responses to a work of literature are irrelevant. Indeed, your personal responses are often a good starting point for the academic work to come. For instance, being puzzled by the unfamiliar cultural assumptions of characters in *The Iliad* can be the first step on the way to a strong analysis. Interrogate your gut reaction. Why are you puzzled? Can you imagine what it would be like to value the things that these ancient warriors value? Does your interpretation of the work change as you learn more about the world from which this epic emerged?

Interrogating your personal responses is the first step in making sure that your argument will be appropriately academic. To help ensure that your responses are critical rather than personal, subject them to the following critical thinking processes: summary, evaluation, analysis, and synthesis.

SUMMARIZE

The first step in thinking critically about any work of literature is to summarize what it is saying. You can construct several different summaries, depending on your goals, but beware: even the most basic of summaries—the plot summary—isn't as simple as it seems. It's difficult to write both economically and descriptively, to discern what's essential to your discussion and what's not.

Consider this: William Shakespeare's *Hamlet* has a very complex plot—the play has a cast of more than thirty characters, and it takes well over four hours to perform it onstage. Perhaps the most widely performed, read, and studied play in English, *Hamlet* is nonetheless notoriously puzzling to first-time readers (or viewers) and well-informed scholars alike. In short, *Hamlet* is one of the most difficult plays to "sum up," and yet the following plot summary does an excellent job:

> Hamlet, a young Danish prince, returns to his home in Elsinore from his university studies abroad to find that his father, the king, is dead. Making matters worse, his uncle has married his mother and assumed the throne. Late one night, a ghost appears to Hamlet, claiming to be his father. The ghost announces that he was murdered—by his own brother, who stole both his wife and his crown. Hamlet vows revenge. However, whether plagued by doubts about the truth of what he has seen, or troubled by the implications for his immortal soul if he kills the new king, Hamlet

becomes lost in a fog of mental turmoil. In his uncertain course toward revenge, Hamlet berates his mother, accidentally kills the king's chief advisor, drives the advisor's daughter (whom he had previously courted) to suicide, and thereby provokes a duel with the advisor's son that eventually leaves the entire court of Elsinore dead. Arriving on the scene as Hamlet utters his last words, the crown prince of Norway claims the Danish throne.

What makes this summary effective? The writer of this summary traces the conflict without being sidetracked by too many of the plot's complications (of which there are many). He sticks to the theme and to the basic conflict/resolution structure. He also makes sure that his sentences are clear. In the end, he produces a summary that is faithful to the play but that doesn't overwhelm the reader with details.

Although you will rarely be asked to include a plot summary in a paper, the exercise of summarizing a literary work in this manner is a useful one. It hones your writing skills, alerts you to gaps in your understanding of the work, and helps you see the structure, conflicts, and themes of the work. But when thinking critically about literature, you needn't limit yourself to plot summary. Equally useful, depending on your purpose, are summaries of a particular work's origins, the author's life and times, similarities to other texts, and the work's reception by its audience and critics (reviews, scholarship, and so on). The point is that summarizing is useful in helping you clarify what you know about a work of literature, laying the foundation for the more complex processes to come.

EVALUATE

Evaluation is an ongoing process. You can evaluate a text the moment you encounter it, and you can continue to evaluate and to reevaluate as you go along. It's important to understand that evaluating a work of literature is different from reacting to it. When you evaluate for an academic purpose, you must find and articulate the reasons for your personal response. What in the text is leading you to respond a certain way? Which influences that are not in the text might be contributing to your response? Watching a performance of *Hamlet*, for instance, you might find yourself becoming impatient with the play's protagonist. What is making you feel this way? The words that Hamlet speaks? The actor's gestures and expressions? The sequence of scenes? Something else? Can you point to a moment in the play when you felt particularly impatient? In asking these questions, you are straddling two intellectual processes: experiencing your own personal response, and analyzing the play.

Evaluation also encourages you to compare a text with other texts that you've read. In a world literature course, this often means comparing texts from all corners of the globe. If you've just read Voltaire's *Candide*, you might ask yourself how it is similar to or notably different from Jonathan Swift's *Gulliver's Travels*. After all, they're both fictional travel narratives written in roughly the same period, though in different countries. You might also ask how either of those texts compares to Chikamatsu Monzaemon's *Love Suicides at Amijima*, written at roughly the same time, but several thousand miles away. Comparisons across time periods can be equally fruitful, especially since most world literature courses cover several centuries. For example, how does *Candide* compare to Molière's *Tartuffe*, both written in France about 100 years apart? Or how does Voltaire compare to twentieth-century French writers like Proust? The possibilities are many, and this process of evaluation will help you discover which aspects of the text are most interesting to you as you investigate them further. Remember: you only need to find one eye-catching idea to put you on the path toward writing a great paper.

ANALYZE

In the analysis stage of constructing an informed argument, your first task is to consider the parts of your topic that most interest you, then examine how these parts relate to one another or to the whole. To analyze *Hamlet* you will want to break the play down by examining particular scenes, particular characters, and particular actions. In short, you'll want to ask: What are the components of this play? How do these components contribute to the work as a whole? To analyze

Kalidasa's *Sakuntala and the Ring of Recollection*, you'll go through a similar process of asking questions that break the play down into its various components.

Ask about the play's structure: What is the purpose of the epigraph in praise of Shiva, or of the prologue at the beginning of Act I?

Ask about the characters and the role they play in the plot: What role does King Duyanta play in the story line? Is he an active player or a passive victim?

Ask about themes: What is the purpose of the nature imagery (flowers, bees, etc.)? What do the curse and its resolution tell you about the relationship in this play between the human and the divine?

Ask about the play's contexts: How does the play reflect the Hindu culture that produced it? Is the play effective in evoking Rasa in its audience? How so?

By asking these questions, you are examining individual components of the play. Your goal is to think about how each of those components functions within the complete work. When you analyze, you break the whole into parts so that you might see the whole differently. When you analyze, you find things to say.

SYNTHESIZE

We've seen that when you analyze, you break a work into its parts. When you synthesize, you look for connections between those parts. In analyzing *Hamlet* you might come up with elements that initially seem disparate. You might have some observations that at first don't seem to jell. Or you might have read various critical perspectives on the play, some of them disagreeing with one another. Now would be the time to consider whether these disparate elements or observations might be reconciled, or synthesized. This intellectual exercise requires that you create an umbrella argument—a larger argument under which several observations and perspectives might stand.

The introductory headnote to *Candide* in *The Norton Anthology of World Literature* provides an excellent example of synthesis. The author of the headnote points out that Voltaire wrote *Candide* to be "deliberately entertaining." The author then discusses the role of humor in the text, and in doing so recounts a lengthy list of comical incidents. It also is pointed out in the headnote that, in spite of the often-outrageous humor, "reality keeps intruding." The author then observes that several comical incidents in the text were inspired by tragic events in real life, such as the 1775 Lisbon earthquake, which had actually killed over 30,000 people. Educated and informed readers therefore not only laugh but are also invited to think seriously about the social and political issues that arise from historical events and their parodies. The author concludes: "The extravagances of the story are therefore uncomfortably matched by the extravagances of real life, and despite the comic lightness of the telling, Voltaire demands that the reader confront these horrors." This conclusion synthesizes the author's many observations about humor and horror, transforming this list of observations into a powerful argument about why humor is an important aspect of *Candide*.

Adopting a Rhetorical Stance

When writing an academic paper, you must consider not only what you want to say but also the audience to whom you're saying it. In other words, it's important to determine not only what you think about a topic but also what your audience is likely to think. What biases does your audience have? What values, expectations, and knowledge do they possess? For whom are you writing, and for what purpose?

When you begin to answer these questions, you have started to reckon with what has been called the "rhetorical stance," which refers to the position you take as a writer in terms of both the subject and the reader of your paper.

CONSIDER YOUR POSITION

Let's first consider your relationship to the topic you're writing about. When you write a paper, you take a stand on a topic. You determine whether you're for or against it, passionate or cool-headed. Because few issues can be reduced to pro and con or black and white, you'll also want to consider the nuances of your position. Finally, you may wish to consider whether or not your position takes a particular critical perspective (e.g., feminist). All of these considerations will enable you to refine your stance on a topic.

To ensure that your stance is appropriately analytical, you should ask yourself some questions. Begin by asking why you've taken this particular position. For instance, why did you find some elements of the work of literature more important than others? Does this prioritizing reflect a bias or preconception on your part? If you dismissed part of the work as boring or unimportant, why did you do so? Do you have personal issues or experiences that might lead you to be impatient with certain elements? Might any part of your response to the literary work cause readers to discount your paper as biased or uncritical? If so, you might want to reconsider your position, or, if you feel strongly about the argument you're trying to make, you will want to carefully plan how you will support that argument with evidence from the text.

CONSIDER YOUR AUDIENCE

Your position on a topic does not, by itself, determine your rhetorical stance. You must also consider your readers. In the college classroom, the audience is usually the professor or your classmates—although occasionally your professor will instruct you to write for a more particular or more general audience. No matter who your readers are, you'll want to consider them carefully before you start to write.

What do you know about your readers and their stance toward your topic? What are they likely to know about the topic? What biases are they likely to have? Moreover, what effect do you hope to have on the readers? Is your aim to be controversial? Informative? Entertaining? Will the readers appreciate or resent your intention?

Once you've determined who your readers are, you will want to consider how you might best reach them. If, for example, you're an authority on a particular subject and you're writing to readers who know little or nothing about that subject, you'll want to take an informative stance. If you aren't yet confident about a topic and you have more questions than answers, you might want to take an inquisitive stance.

In any case, when you're deciding on a rhetorical stance, choose one that allows you to be sincere. You don't want to take an authoritative stance on a subject if you cannot be confident about what you're saying. On the other hand, you don't want to avoid taking a position on a subject; readers are very often frustrated by writers who refuse to take a clear stance. What if you are of two minds on a subject? Declare that to the reader. Make ambivalence your clear rhetorical stance.

Finally, don't write simply to please your professor. Though some professors find it flattering to discover that all of their students share their positions on a subject, most of us are hoping that your argument will engage us by telling us something new about your topic—even if that "something new" is simply a fresh emphasis on a minor detail. Moreover, it's impossible for you to replicate the ideal paper that exists in your professor's head. When you try, you risk having your analysis compared to your professor's own. Is that really what you want?

Considering Tone and Style

So now you understand what's required of you in an academic paper. You need to be analytical. You need to create an informed argument. You need to consider your relationship to the topic and to the reader. But what about finding an appropriate academic tone and style?

The tone and style of academic writing might at first seem intimidating. But that needn't be the case. Professors want students to write clearly and intelligently on matters that they, the students, care about. What professors don't want is imitation scholarship—that is, exalted gibberish that no one cares to read. If the student didn't care to write the paper, the professor probably won't care to read it. The tone of an academic paper, then, must be inviting to the reader, even while it maintains an appropriate academic style.

Remember that professors are human beings, capable of boredom, laughter, irritation, and awe. They have lives outside of their duties as teachers, and they don't appreciate having their time wasted any more than you do. Understand that you're writing to a person who will be delighted when you make your point clearly, concisely, and persuasively. Understand, too, that she will be less delighted if you have inflated your prose, pumped up your page count, or tried to impress her by using terms that you didn't take the time to understand. (For more on how to craft an appropriate but engaging academic tone and style, see Chapter 7, "Attending to Style," later in this guide.)

2

Kinds of Writing About World Literature

Now that you have a sense of what it means to write an academic paper, you can think about what you need to do to write successfully about world literature. The study of world literature is a diverse and fascinating field. Scholars who write in this discipline write not only about particular works of literature but also about the authors, the cultural and historical contexts surrounding those works, and the history of the various genres of world literature. Let's turn our attention now to some of the kinds of papers that you will be asked to write in a world literature course.

Textual Analysis of a Work of Literature

One of the most common approaches to writing about world literature is textual analysis. Textual analysis requires the reader to break down the work into its different parts and to discuss how each part adds up to create the whole. This process is similar to taking apart a tractor in a field: you lay out the parts, try to understand the function and purpose of each one, and then put the parts back together. After doing this, you will no doubt understand much better how the tractor works, and you will be able to talk about its workings with precision and clarity. When it comes to taking apart a literary text, the particular pieces you're dealing with depend on the text you're analyzing. In a short poem you may need to look at rhythm, rhyme schemes, and the poet's use of rhetorical figures of speech. In novels or short stories you'll want to look at the characters, settings, motifs, and conflicts. In plays you'll need to look at characters' behavior, stage directions, instances of dramatic irony, and possibly soliloquies or other lengthy speeches. In all cases, you should think about the themes of the work, as well as the overall effect of reading the text, but be aware: themes are often best understood and written about when you view them through one of the afore-mentioned textual elements. In other words, as the author of a textual analysis paper, your goal is to choose one of these elements and examine in detail how that element contributes to the major themes or overall effect of the text.

Although some professors provide detailed instructions in their assignments—which topic to cover, which elements to discuss, and possibly even which part of the work to analyze—others permit students to choose the literary work and the overall topic they wish to discuss. Thus you might write a paper about characterization in Anton Chekhov's *The Cherry*

Orchard or the portrayal of time and memory in Marcel Proust's *Swann's Way*. Each of these topics clearly focuses on describing and interpreting the effectiveness of a single element or technique in a single work.

Contextual Analysis of a Work of Literature

A literary work's concerns are almost always oriented toward society—humans living among humans. To thoroughly understand a literary work, you must therefore consider the work's social, cultural, and political contexts. Understanding the context in which a work of literature is produced and enjoyed is especially important in a world literature course, where you are being asked to interpret texts from cultures across the globe.

To uncover a work's cultural or political arguments, you will want to undertake a contextual analysis. Contextual analysis involves examining the relationship between a work and its contexts: the social norms and political environment of the culture in which it was written, the historical events before or during the author's life, the literary tradition and popular culture in the region at that time, and so on. Four useful questions you can ask yourself to find fruitful approaches to a contextual analysis paper follow:

1. How is this text a *product* of its historical or cultural context? In other words, what historical or cultural forces conspired to create this particular work of literature? For instance,

for almost a century before Chikamatsu Monzaemon wrote *Love Suicides at Amijima*, Japan had been experiencing a population shift toward urban centers. The relative prosperity of the middle and working classes created a demand for popular entertainment. Chikamatsu's *Bunraku* productions filled that demand, providing insight into the lives, customs, and values of the people of Osaka at that time.

2. How does the text *reflect* its cultural context? In other words, in what ways does the text serve as a historical document that allows readers to reconstruct the society in which it was composed? Consider *The Epic of Gilgamesh*, which exemplifies this idea quite well. Though most of its key events are clearly mythic, the text illustrates several cultural values that are important to the society that produced it: fraternal affection; the power of sexuality; the importance of the distinction between civilization and wild savagery; and the idea that since biological immortality is impossible, a form of immortality can be achieved by creating lasting works on earth.

3. How did the text *influence* future historical events or inspire social change? *Candide* (along with many other texts from the European Enlightenment period) is often credited with helping to inspire the American and French Revolutions near the end of the eighteenth century. If you peruse historical documents associated with those events—for example, *Common Sense*, the Declaration of

Independence, or the Declaration of the Rights of Man and Citizen—you might find similarities between those documents' ideologies and the ideas from *Candide*. Which specific parts of the novel provide this potential influence?

4. How does the text *comment* upon recent history? To what purpose? A classic example of cultural commentary is Chinua Achebe's novel *Things Fall Apart*, in which Achebe critiques the colonization of Africa. What, precisely, is Achebe condemning in the political systems that he critiques? How is this critique rendered in the novel?

Once you've determined how a work is speaking to, about, or from its historical and cultural contexts, you will want to consider the work's political views. Granted, not all literature expresses a clear political ideology. Nevertheless, even when a work avoids expressing overtly political or ideological messages, it cannot help but convey subtle attitudes about the social arrangements and problems portrayed within. As you try to sort out a work's political argument, you might consider the following questions:

Does the work of literature seem to espouse a particular set of beliefs and values?

Is the work bringing competing beliefs and values into conflict with each other? If so, what is the writer telling us, explicitly and implicitly, about these beliefs and values?

Does the work seem explicitly political? Or, is it more generally concerned with portraying a social problem?

Does any character in the work consistently embody a particular worldview? What happens to this character? Are we meant to sympathize with him or her?

Knowing what you know about the history of the work and the time in which it was written, can you say whether or not the work is responding to a major cultural crisis—for example, a war, a famine, a political revolution, a grave injustice—**that the author would have been concerned about?**

How was the work first received when it was published? What does this early reception tell you about the work's relationship to the prevailing values of the culture in which it was written and performed?

Comparison Papers

Sometimes a professor will ask you to do a formal analysis paper comparing and/or contrasting two or more works of literature. A comparative study requires that you look at specific elements in each text and compare or contrast their qualities. Two strategies tend to produce good results. First, you might take two things assumed to be very similar but then go on to show important differences between the two (for example, comparing the story "The Death of Atsumori" from the epic *Heike Monogatari* to Zeami Motokiyo's play *Atsumori*). Second, you might take two things assumed to be very dissimilar and show important similarities (for example, describing how an important religious text, the *Bhagavad Gita*, and a heroic epic, *Beowulf*, both dramatize the tensions between violence, loyalties, and revenge). Whatever strategy you choose, remember: for a compare/contrast paper to be effective, the writer must be sure to limit the comparison to the most salient points. A paper that articulates carefully a few important comparisons or contrasts and analyzes their significance will fare much better than a paper that simply presents a laundry list of similarities and differences with no analysis or commentary.

The following hypothetical paper assignments show how the comparative approach is well suited to producing insightful and interesting papers:

1. Compare Sophocles' *Oedipus the King* to Euripides' *Medea* with respect to human relationships and dynamics with the gods. How does Euripides' worldview differ from Sophocles' worldview?

2. Compare and contrast the central character in the *Bhagavad Gita* with the eponymous hero of *Beowulf*. What do the differences between these two heroes tell us about the cultures in which they were composed (India during the first century B.C.E. and ninth-century Anglo-Saxon England)?

3. Compare Derek Walcott's *Omeros* to Homer's *Odyssey* in terms of conventions of epic poetry. Which conventions does Walcott keep and which does he ignore? Of those that he retains, does he modify them in any way? How does the use of epic conventions suit the needs of this particular text?

Note that the first assignment asks you to compare between two works that were written within the same cultural milieu, by two playwrights who were alive at the same time and aware of each other's work. The differences between their two plays thus arise from the playwrights' individual styles and worldviews. The second assignment asks you to use two heroic figures as windows into the respective cultures in which the works about them were composed. The third assignment asks you to compare particular textual elements from two works created thousands of years and thousands of miles apart. In this case you are being asked to examine the nature of literary influence and the way one author can build on such influence to make his writing relevant in a new social and geopolitical context.

Writing About Adaptation

Since works of literature resonate strongly with their readers, many works are adapted to new forms to reach new audiences. Although the most common mode of adaptation is turning a work of literature into a film, adaptation can take many unusual and interesting forms. Samuel Taylor Coleridge's poem "The Rime of the Ancient Mariner," for example, was adapted into a heavy metal song by Iron Maiden. *Candide* was turned into an opera by Lillian Hellman and Leonard Bernstein. The Brothers Quay created a stop-motion animation short film based loosely on the beginning to *The Epic Gilgamesh*.

Writing a paper about an adapted work is typically a form of comparison paper—you are comparing the original text to the adaptation (or, sometimes, to multiple adaptations). As with any comparison paper, merely writing a laundry list of similarities and differences won't be very interesting—for you or for your reader. Rather, you should try to examine the significance of the differences you've observed, particularly any differences produced by the new form. Iron Maiden's "Rime of the Ancient Mariner," for instance, includes a lengthy pause with a voiceover between two verses. What effect does this adaptation have on your impression of the story? How does it contribute to the presentation of the piece? Since it is a musical adaptation, the artists have control over tempo and volume in ways that Coleridge does not in his written version. Does the band successfully take advantage of the adapted form?

In addition to the differences, you should also pay attention to notable similarities. Most of the Iron Maiden adaptation tells the story of the mariner using words and phrases that do not actually appear in Coleridge's poem. Nevertheless, a few sections quote the poem verbatim. Why is that? Why leave those sections entirely unchanged while modifying everything else?

Once you've determined the differences and similarities between the two works, ask yourself two key questions. First, is the adaptation true to the original text? For instance, if the original text has an underlying political, social, or moral message, does the adaptation successfully present a similar message? Second, what is the purpose of the adaptation? Is it merely a matter of reaching a different audience? Does the adapted version change or update the message of the original in some way? You'll want to articulate as clearly as possible what that particular adaptation is trying to accomplish.

The list of adaptations you could write about is long— especially when you consider that not every adaptation uses the same title as the original literary work. Disney's animated film *The Lion King* is an adaptation of Shakespeare's *Hamlet*. New versions of older works put into modern settings are sometimes not really adaptations but, rather, retellings or new visions of an older work. The film *Bedazzled* (2000) is essentially a retelling of the Faust myth, as are countless other books and films based on the notion of a Faustian bargain. The multiple adaptations and retellings of *Faust*—in forms as varied as stage drama, opera, film, and more—provide ample opportunities for comparison papers.

Translation

Translating a work from one language to another is really just a form of adaptation. In world literature courses, many of the texts you read are works that were originally written in languages other than English. Inevitably, any two translations of a work will be different, sometimes radically different, from each other. Evaluating a work of literature by comparing various translations can lead you to interesting, eye-opening discoveries. If you are able to read the text in its original language, you will be able to evaluate the relationship between the original and its English translation.

Essay Exams

Not everything you write in a world literature course will involve writing papers per se. In fact, in many world literature classrooms, there are no formal writing requirements. Instead, many courses use in-class "essay exams," where you are expected to write a short essay in class during a timed examination period. Most of the advice in this book still applies to essay exams, but you may need to make a few adjustments to your writing process.

There are two important differences between an essay exam and a take-home essay: you likely won't be able to do any research or use any outside sources, and you have a time limit. These differences require a slightly different approach to the assignment.

First you need to consider the type of essay you're writing. In some cases your professor will give a specific essay prompt on an exam, but you also might find that the prompt is so broad that you're basically coming up with your own topic. Take a moment and look back at the kinds of writing assignments described earlier. You'll probably notice right away that some of these types of papers lend themselves to in-class writing better than others. Textual analysis will work quite well, because all you need is your memory and your knowledge of the primary text. Comparative analysis is also a reasonable possibility, because you will surely have a strong working knowledge of more than one primary text that you read for the class.

Contextual analysis might work, but you need to keep in mind that you won't be able to do any research, so in this case you are limited to the knowledge of history, culture, or other relevant information that you already have when you enter the classroom. However, if you happen to know a lot about, for instance, early eighteenth-century Japan and for your final exam you have to write an essay on Chikamatsu Monzaemon's *Love Suicides at Amijima*, then you're in luck! You already have the tools to incorporate historical context into your essay.

Except in unusual circumstances, writing about adaptation is probably not a good choice for an essay test. Reading (or viewing, or listening to) the adapted form of the work is essentially a specific form of research, which you won't be able to perform during the exam. So unless you have an exceptionally strong knowledge of, for example, a film version of the primary text about which you are writing, it's probably better to choose a different essay form.

The other factor you need to consider for essay exams is the time limit, which should affect your preparatory work. You have two goals for your prep work: do it quickly, and make it effective so you can also write the essay quickly. Obviously when you're in a timed environment, you don't want to waste a lot of time generating and organizing your ideas before you actually start writing the essay. If you do, you run the risk of not having enough time to finish. On the other hand, you don't want to just jump right into the essay without any forethought. If you perform your preparatory work well, it should make the essay-writing process go much faster and will end up saving you time.

In the next chapter we will present some techniques for generating ideas: brainstorming, freewriting, a discovery draft, five Ws and an H, and so on. If you are taking a course in which the essay test is the primary writing requirement, read the descriptions of these idea-generating techniques with a critical eye. Some of these techniques are more useful for essay tests than others, mostly because of how long they will take you to perform. Brainstorming (page 41), for example, can be fairly quick, so it's a good strategy to employ when taking an essay test. The journalistic "five Ws and an H" technique (page 48) is also fast, and it gives you a specific goal. Even tagmemics (page 49) or a very brief run through the topoi (page 51) could prove useful. Use whichever method you've found to be quick and efficient.

After you come up with some ideas, it might be tempting to start writing—after all, you don't want to waste any time, right? But you should resist that temptation. You'll probably find that it's actually more time-efficient not to start writing until you have a plan. So take the ideas from your brainstorming or other exercises and organize them into a coherent outline. You needn't produce something fancy. Just make a quick sketch to see how the essay will take shape, and then start writing. With the outline to guide you, the writing process should go much more quickly, although the fact that it will end up saving you time is actually just an added bonus. The real reason to use an outline is that it will improve the quality (the coherence and the clarity) of your essay, and it will keep you from getting lost in your many good ideas.

It's important to keep in mind that even though in-class writing and essay tests will feel different from regular essay assignments, the differences we've just discussed are really the only major distinctions. Almost everything else is the same, and the other pieces of advice you'll read about in this book—such as developing your thesis, organizing your argument, arranging your paragraphs, and making your essay coherent—all still apply.

One final note: on an essay test, it's often a good idea to plan out how you'll spend your time at the beginning of the exam period. Let's suppose you have a mid-term exam in a 50-minute class session. Your professor gives you three prompts and tells you to choose one. Your plan for the exam might look like this:

2 minutes: think about the prompts and pick one
5 minutes: brainstorm
7 minutes: nutshell from the brainstorm; come up with a working thesis
7 minutes: create a detailed outline
25 minutes: write the essay
4 minutes: reread what you've written and make revisions

Whichever schedule you put yourself on, make sure you dedicate enough time to preparatory work and outlining. It will make writing the essay a lot easier.

In some situations, completing detailed preparatory work may also have a hidden benefit. If you unfortunately run out of time before completing the essay, your brainstorming notes and outline will help show your professor what you would have written if the exam period were longer. An outline, of course, is not a substitute for an actual essay. Nevertheless, some instructors may be more generous in their grading if your preparatory work shows that you understand the material and that you likely would have written a high-quality essay if you had had more time. Such grading decisions are up to individual instructors, and we cannot guarantee that your instructor will give partial credit for a good outline—but providing an outline probably won't hurt.

3

Generating Ideas

In some ways writing about literature is similar to writing on any subject: you must choose a topic, generate ideas, research your topic, craft a thesis, structure your argument, and find the proper tone. But each of these more general tasks requires you to perform some tasks that are specific to the study of world literature. For instance, you must know how to read literature imaginatively and analytically, how to use specialized language appropriately, and how to use research resources effectively. The following section combines general advice with suggestions specific to the study of world literature, with the aim of helping you produce better papers for your world literature class.

Reading Critically/Reading Creatively

As we've said earlier, literature is a social phenomenon. However, the act of reading is usually an individual pursuit. While there are many advantages to the individual nature of reading (you can read at your own pace, wherever and whenever you like), there are some disadvantages as well. When you have social interactions with other people, your communication will involve much more than just words; for example, hand gestures, facial expressions, tone of voice, and other behaviors convey meaning. When you read, however, you don't have the benefit of that additional information. Authors therefore use other techniques to help convey their meaning. It is your job as a reader to identify and decipher the clues the author leaves for you.

READING CRITICALLY

Critical reading is essentially looking beyond what a text *says* to discover what it *means*. Critical reading begins with the understanding that the words you see on the page are only a starting point, and that other information is available to you. You should examine the way those words are presented, as well as the choices the author makes in crafting the text: language and tone, figures of speech, humor, rhythm, and so on. You should also try to determine what purpose these textual elements serve. A few simple examples follow.

Identify irony

In the first chapter of Voltaire's *Candide*, the narrator provides Candide's thoughts about the home of Baron Thunder-ten-tronkch: "The Baron was one of the most mighty lords in Westphalia because his castle had a door and windows. His great hall was even hung with a tapestry." At first glance this description appears to be filled with high praise, especially since it begins by describing the baron as "one of the most mighty lords" of his region. However, if you read a little closer and think about the details of the passage, you'll notice that the text is actually implying the opposite—the baron is not particularly wealthy or powerful (at least not by aristocratic standards). The best thing the narrator can say about the castle is that it has a door and windows, just like every other castle in Europe. Its decorations are not described as including lavish artwork, jewelry, reliquaries, and the like. Rather, the castle has only one tapestry. Determining that the "praise" heaped upon the baron's home is ironic is an important part of understanding this chapter. Think about the purpose this irony serves. In this case the irony indicates that the protagonist is naively optimistic: he thinks the best of his situation regardless of any evidence to the contrary. Understanding this characterization of Candide will help you understand his thought process and decision making throughout the text. In this way the irony of the passage provides a key to help you read the rest of the work. You now know that the narrator often provides information ironically—and you can read accordingly.

Identify implied information

Very often, authors will provide information about characters or events via clues that you must decipher. In James Joyce's short story "Araby," the young narrator spends a few hours waiting for his uncle to come home. The narrator describes his eventual arrival: "At nine o'clock I heard my uncle's latch-key in the halldoor. I heard him talking to himself and heard the hallstand rocking when it had received the weight of his overcoat. I could interpret these signs." Try a quick exercise and answer the following questions: Why is the narrator's uncle late coming home? Where was he? How can you tell?

READING CREATIVELY

Along with reading critically, you should also practice reading creatively. Often, texts will imply information or build on abstract ideas, and you must imaginatively interpret the contents of the work in order to understand it. Here are a few examples:

Interpret textual details imaginatively

Again in the first chapter of Voltaire's *Candide*, the Baron's daughter Cunégonde has an interesting experience: "One day, as Cunégonde was walking near the castle in the little woods that they called a park, she saw Dr. Pangloss in the underbrush; he was giving a lesson in experimental physics to her mother's maid, a very attractive and obedient brunette. As Miss Cunégonde had a natural bent for the sciences, she watched breathlessly the repeated experiments which were going on; she saw clearly the doctor's sufficient reason, observed both cause and effect, and returned to the house in a distracted and pensive frame of mind, yearning for knowledge and dreaming that she might be the sufficient reason of young Candide." If you read the first sentence of this passage critically, you'll find clues that show Pangloss is definitely having sexual intercourse with the maid in the bushes. The fact that he's in the underbrush to begin with indicates he's trying to hide, and the information about the maid's appearance would not be especially important if he were actually teaching her about experimental physics. Knowing what the characters are actually doing here, you can envision the scene as the rest of it is told through euphemisms such as "sufficient reason" and "cause and effect." You'll know exactly why Cunégonde goes back to the house looking for Candide.

Imagine the world of the text

Jorge Luis Borges's short story "The Garden of Forking Paths" involves a fictional book by the deceased writer Ts'ui Pen. In this passage a character explains how this book is unlike all others: "In all fictional works, each time a man is confronted with several alternatives, he chooses one and eliminates the others; in the fiction of Ts'ui Pen, he chooses—simultaneously—all of them. He *creates*, in this way, diverse futures, diverse times which themselves also proliferate and fork." The world of this fictional book is one in which multiple realities exist simultaneously. This world is very different from the world we all inhabit, and it requires creative thinking to understand it. But once you are able to imagine this world, you should be able to apply that same creativity toward analyzing its role within the text.

Immersing Yourself in the World of the Text

Many texts you read in a world literature class will come from countries or time periods you don't know much about. A little background information about the historical and cultural contexts of the work will help your understanding of it tremendously. This background investigation doesn't have to involve extensive, time-consuming research—even just a little bit of pertinent information will be useful. If you don't really know where to begin, a good starting point is to use the advice from the previous section and try to imagine the text. Start by finding basic information that will help you create that mental picture: *How should the characters dress?* Fashion choices might be different for wealthy characters than for poor characters, or they might differ due to the characters' jobs, social standing, and so on. *How do people in this society talk?* Consider the language characters are speaking, as well as the patterns and habits of discourse they exhibit. *What is normal behavior?* Investigate dominant social values or mores. Consider whether characters act in accordance with those values or whether they violate them.

If you want to delve further into the world of the text, you might want to look at some of the questions raised in the section "Contextual Analysis of a Work of Literature" in Chapter 2 in this guide. Or just start with anything that seems interesting and see where your research takes you. Try to have fun with it—one of the great pleasures of a world literature course is the opportunity to learn about far-off places and people you might otherwise never know anything about.

Using Specialized Language

Think back to the dinner party we talked about at the beginning of the book. Just as it's a good idea to familiarize yourself with the ongoing conversation before jumping in, it's also a good idea to make sure that when you start speaking, you understand the terms of this particular conversation. Virtually every industry, discipline, or activity has its own vocabulary, and literature is no different. Learning and using appropriate terminology will make your job as a scholarly writer much easier.

Start with the basics. If you're writing about a play, be sure to refer to it as a play, not as a novel or short story. Learn to recognize common, frequently used figures of speech such as metaphor, metonymy, and simile; learn the differences between them and when to use them. You certainly don't need to learn every literary term all at once (or ever), but as you read more, you'll be exposed to additional literary techniques, and you should make an effort to learn them as you come across them. Remember how they differ from terms you already know so you can use the correct terminology when you write.

For more complicated terminology, let your instructor guide you. If you read Zeami's play *Atsumori*, your instructor might tell you about Noh drama. You may use this term much less frequently than "metaphor" or "irony," but if you plan to write a paper about *Atsumori*, it's a good idea to have a basic understanding of Noh drama, and you may wish to do additional research. If you learn about the differences between various forms of Japanese drama, such as Noh, Kabuki, and Bunraku, then it will become easier to talk and write about each of them. The bottom line is you should learn whatever terms you need in order to sound persuasive when you join the conversation at the dinner party.

Generating Ideas

While reading a work of literature, you will usually come up with some ideas worth writing about. But what if you've read the work a few times and you still haven't found anything that you feel is worth exploring? Or what if you've found an idea for writing, but you haven't yet discovered how you might develop that idea? In any of these situations you might want to take the time to try one of the following strategies for generating ideas.

CONVERSATION

After experiencing cultural events on our own time—for instance, after seeing a movie or attending a concert—we typically talk about it with others as soon as we leave the venue. Those conversations often leave us thinking about the movie or concert in new and interesting ways. Similarly, conversations with your classmates about the works of literature that you've read for class can help you discover what's interesting about a particular work. Note, however, that the kinds of conversations that we have with our friends—which are often freewheeling, opinionated, and more emotional than intellectual—mark just the beginning of scholarly inquiry. Still, talking with friends can be useful in exploring differences of opinion and in encouraging you to articulate and back up your point of view.

BRAINSTORMING

Another way to formulate ideas is to brainstorm. Brainstorming is useful because it is a quick and efficient way of laying out what you know about a subject. By brainstorming, you might also see what you don't know about a topic, which might move you to read and think further.

Suppose you have decided to brainstorm for a paper on *The Epic of Gilgamesh*. You might make a list like the one that follows:

The Epic of Gilgamesh
- is an epic poem;
- is about an ancient Sumerian king;

- involves a lot of sex;
- involves battles with some crazy-looking beasts/ monsters;
- emphasizes the difference between gods and humans;
- emphasizes the difference between civilized people and wild barbarians;
- contains some interesting similarities to the Old Testament (the snake, the flood) but was written much earlier;
- involves a failed search for immortality;
- isn't as fun or interesting to read as Homer's *Odyssey*.

As this list illustrates, brainstorming is an informal strategy for invention in which you jot down, as quickly as you can, ideas concerning your topic. The ideas don't have to be connected—though sometimes looking for connections will yield a paper topic. For instance, you might want to write a paper arguing that while *The Epic of Gilgamesh* is very much of its time and calls attention to issues important to ancient Mesopotamian culture, it seems fresh and contemporary even now because one of the themes at the center of the work— coming to terms with one's own mortality—will always be with us.

Remember that you can also stop at any point in the writing process to brainstorm, especially when you feel that you're stuck or that you have to fill in some gaps in your argument. In short, when you brainstorm you freely explore your topic without the pressure of structure, grammar, or style. In the process, ideas for an essay (or a paragraph, or even a footnote) can evolve unhindered.

FREEWRITING

Freewriting is similar to brainstorming in that it is a quick and informal way to develop an idea. But whereas brainstorming most often involves making a list of ideas, freewriting requires that you try to elaborate on these ideas by writing about them, without paying close attention to syntax or grammar. In this way, freewriting can get you "unstuck" when coming up with ideas is difficult.

Here's an example (and note that this freewriting, since it is meant for the writer's eyes only, is very informal—with spelling, grammar, and punctuation errors intact).

OK, so I just finished Samuel Beckett's Endgame and, wow, I'm supposed to write a paper on it but I have no idea what I'm going to say. It was easy enough to read, but half the time I was wondering what the heck was the point of all the talking, and when was something going to happen. but still i gotta come up with something. where to start? maybe i should begin with the point in the play where I realized that it's supposed to be funny in places, like when Nagg tells Nell "Our hearing hasn't failed" and she replise "Our what?" Up to that point, I didn't know what to make of the play. I even worried that it was going to be a long, depressing play. And sure, it is depressing.

But it's also funny at times, in a dark way, but still funny. lots of the humor is about words and what they mean, and how the things we say don't connect to the things we do, like Clov always telling Hamm "I'll leave you," but he never does. Even at the end of the play he's dressed to go but he just stands near the door watching Hamm until the end. At the beginning of the play, I wouldn't know what to make of that. But after awhile, I actually laughed when Clov would say "I'll leave you, I have things to do." The end when he's just standing there is a little sad, though. So, it's funny in a way, but clearly it's dark, and words seem to be at the heart of what makes the play dark, too. And the "action" of the play is also a sad (but sometimes funny) parody of real action in the form of words. I didn't even realize it as I was doing it, but I just put quotation marks around the word "action". I guess that's becuse there's really not much action at all. Infact, most of the play seems like it's about inaction. Like Nagg and Nell—they cant move at all. The whole idea of not going anywhere seems like it's really important in the play. That must be why Clov keeps talking about leaving but never doing it. So maybe I can write about that—inaction, people not moving, not doing stuff. It's so different from most plays I've read. hmmmm. i guess this was a pretty successful freewrite. all i had to do was push buttons and some ideas popped out. pushing buttons is a lot more fun than just sitting and staring at a blank screen.

DISCOVERY DRAFT

A discovery draft is another strategy for coming up with or developing your ideas. A discovery draft is similar to freewriting in that you can write freely, with little thought to the structure and the development of your ideas for the time being. You can also forget about matters of syntax and style. However, writing a discovery draft is different from freewriting in that a discovery draft makes a conscious attempt to focus on and develop an idea or a cluster of ideas. In other words, a discovery draft is like freewriting with an agenda. And because you have an agenda, a discovery draft tends to be more structured than freewriting, and to be written more or less coherently, in complete sentences.

Think of writing a discovery draft as writing a letter to a friend about your paper. You might first summarize, for your friend's benefit, the literary work and the issues it presents. You might then raise questions about the work. You might challenge the author on certain points. You might point out a certain part of the work that you found compelling. You might address and then work out any confusion that you have about the work's plot or characterization. In writing the discovery draft you might have an aha! moment in which you see something you hadn't seen before and break off mid-sentence to explore it.

In a sense, the aha! moment is the point of the discovery draft. When writing the discovery draft, your thoughts are focused on your topic. You're giving language to your questions and observations. In this process, the mind almost always stumbles across something new—it makes a discovery. And with this discovery, a paper is often launched.

An example of the beginning of a discovery draft follows:

In Endgame, a lot of words and phrases are repeated very often throughout the play. Sometimes even entire mini-conversations are repeated. The most obvious repeated words are "end" and "finish," or variations of those words, like "ending," or "finished." This repetition must be connected to the title, Endgame. Both the title and the constant use of the words "end" and "finish" seem to suggest that the characters are just waiting for their lives to end, not really doing anything about it. In fact, they're not really doing much of anything at all.

Another repeated phrase is Clov's ongoing threat "I'll leave you." Sometimes he follows it up with "I have things to do." Hamm always seems skeptical. He's skeptical both that Clov will leave and that he has anything he needs to do.

The phrase that really sticks out is Hamm asking for his pain-killer, which he does a lot. Clov always responds that it's not time for it yet, until the last time Hamm asks. Then Clov tells him there aren't any pain-killers left. It seems like a metaphor—there's no way to escape the pain.

All of this repetition must mean something. Let's look closer at one of the examples. As I already said, Clov is always telling Hamm he's going to leave because he has "things to do," but he never really does anything except talk to Hamm. Even at the end of the play, when he finally acts like he might actually leave, he just stands by the door, watching and waiting. He never really does much of anything, and neither does Hamm. Furthermore, since it seems like there aren't any other people anywhere, the situation Hamm and Clov find themselves in seems to represent Beckett's view of the human condition: everyone is waiting to die. That's why the characters keep using the words "end" and "finish:" they're just waiting to die. The pain-killer incident really hammers home the point: There's no point in doing anything, because all people are basically just waiting to die, and there's no escaping that fate.

Notice that this is more formal than a freewriting exercise. It always uses complete sentences and correct grammar, and it follows a logical train of thought. However, it's still not nearly as formal as a paper that you would hand in to your professor. It uses casual, colloquial language, and it doesn't state ideas as strongly as it might (because as you write a discovery draft, you're often still trying to figure out what, exactly, those ideas are). Also notice that the discovery draft uses some of the thoughts that showed up in the freewrite. Freewriting helps you find ideas that might be useful in your paper; the discovery draft helps you figure out how they're useful and what you might say about them. A student who writes this freewriting exercise and this discovery draft about *Endgame* is now well on the way to a solid, working thesis.

FIVE Ws AND AN H

Journalism has provided us with perhaps the simplest and most familiar way of coming up with a topic: simply ask questions such as *who, what, when, where, why,* and *how.* Answering these questions initially doesn't seem very hard—at least until one gets to the *why* and *how.* Then it gets tricky.

Let's use this method to try to generate ideas for a paper on Chinua Achebe's *Things Fall Apart.* Maybe when you were reading the novel you got interested in the use of Igbo proverbs and aphorisms in the text, so you have a topic you want to explore. Now begin your interrogation:

Where in the novel do you find aphorisms? Mark the sections.
What are the aphorisms? Write down each specific proverb
    and what you think it means.
Who is reciting the proverbs, and who is listening to them?
    Consider not only who might be listening within the
    text but who is listening *beyond* the text. Who are the
    book's various audiences?
When in the novel do the aphorisms appear? What is happen-
    ing in those moments? What purpose do the aphorisms
    serve at this particular moment?
How is the proverb presented? Is it spoken by a character? Is
    it part of the narration? How does it comment on the
    rest of the scene, or on the novel as a whole?
After thinking about the answers to the aforementioned

questions, ask yourself: *Why do aphorisms and proverbs play such a prominent role in* Things Fall Apart?

The last question is a tough one. But it's precisely when you have difficulty answering a *why* question that a real paper is beginning to emerge. When the answer comes too easily, you're on familiar ground, so you're probably not saying anything interesting. Cultivate a taste for confusion. Then cultivate a strategy for clearing up confusion. Only when you ask a question that initially confuses you can real thinking and real writing begin.

TAGMEMICS

Tagmemics is a system that allows you to look at a single object from three different perspectives. One of these perspectives (or even all three) can help you determine a subject for writing. By extending an analogy regarding the different ways physicists think about light, tagmemics involves seeing your topic

as a particle (as a thing in itself);
as a wave (as a thing changing over time);
as part of a field (as a thing in its context).

Suppose you want to write a paper on Bertolt Brecht's *The Good Woman of Szechwan*. If you use tagmemics as a system of invention, you will begin by looking at the play as a thing in itself. In other words, you will do a close textual reading, paying attention to the words on the page and the implications those words have for a staged production.

Next you might consider how the play has changed over time. How was the play received in its day? How does this reception compare to current assessments of the play? Research notable productions of the play. Which elements of the play have been emphasized in each production? How has the approach to the play changed over time?

Finally, consider *The Good Woman of Szechwan* as a thing in context. Relate it to its culture, to its moment in time. Work on *The Good Woman* was begun in 1938, while Brecht was in exile from his native Germany in Finland. The play was finally finished and staged in 1943, by which time Brecht was in the United States, where he would remain until 1947. What was happening in the world between 1938 and 1943? Most significantly, Nazi Germany during this period finally launched what would become known as World War II. Germany was also perpetrating the mass killing of Jews and other "undesirables" within its sphere of influence. By early 1943 the Soviet Union had defeated the Germans at Stalingrad—a victory that turned the tide of Hitler's campaign on the Eastern Front, and in the war overall. Might these events be reflected in the play in some way? How? And why?

ARISTOTLE'S TOPOI

As one of the fathers of rhetoric, Aristotle worked to formalize a system for conceiving, organizing, and expressing ideas. We're concerned here with what Aristotle called the "topoi"—a system of specific strategies for invention. Think of the topoi as a series of questions that you might ask of a work of literature—questions that might lead you to interesting paper topics. The topoi are especially helpful when you're asked to explore a topic that seems very broad. Consider, for instance, how using the topoi can help you write a paper on the importance of Aimé Césaire's *Notebook of a Return to the Native Land* to late twentieth-century understandings of postcolonial literature.

Use definition

You can use definition in two ways to come up with or develop a topic. First you might look at "genus," which Aristotle explains as defining a general idea within specific limits. For example, you could define "postcolonial" with the intent of showing how *Notebook* epitomizes a postcolonial mentality or how the book illustrates the postcolonial condition.

The second way to use definition is to think in terms of division. In other words, try to think of your subject in terms of its parts. For example, identify the aspects of *Notebook* that are most significant with regard to postcolonial politics, or with regard to other well-known works of literature by post-colonial authors.

Use comparison

You can generate ideas by making comparisons in two ways. The first is to look for similarities and/or differences. For example, you might determine how *Notebook* stands apart from other important works of postcolonial poetry, such as Derek Walcott's *Omeros*.

The second method is to compare degree. In other words, you might consider how something is more or less than something else in some particular regard, or perhaps better or worse. For example, is *Notebook* a better representation of Caribbean postcolonial thought than *Omeros*, or works by Jamaica Kincaid? Why or why not? What if you expand that comparison beyond the Caribbean to other parts of the world?

Explore relationships

Aristotle determined four ways of exploring relationships as a strategy for coming up with ideas for writing. The first is to consider either the cause of your subject or its effects. For example, you might research the effects that *Notebook* has had on subsequent poetry, postcolonial or otherwise.

Second, you might consider a subject's antecedent and consequences. In other words, you might ask this question of your subject: If this, then what? For example, if *Notebook* hadn't been written, would poetry or postcolonial literature today look any different?

Third, you might examine contraries, or make an argument

by proving its opposite. An example is to say that war is bad in order to convey the idea that peace is good. Along these lines, you might argue that *Notebook* is a significant work of postcolonial poetry by showing how others miss the mark.

Finally, you might look for contradictions, incompatible statements, or controversy. For example, some critics feel that *Notebook* is one of the greatest poems of the twentieth century; others feel that it's overrated, too confusing and abstract, and deliberately provocative. You can explore the controversy and stake a claim of your own.

Examine circumstances

In seeking an idea for a paper, you can examine circumstances in two ways. The first is to consider the possible and the impossible. Sometimes you can construct an interesting argument by considering what's possible and what's not. For example, imagine if it is possible for Césaire to have written *Notebook* if he had not lived for several years in France. How might his perspective and his art be different if he never left Martinique?

The second strategy is to consider the past or to look to the future. For example, in what ways does *Notebook* influence poets (or other writers) today? In what ways was it influenced by the long history of poetry, or the relatively shorter history of postcolonial literature, and in what ways does it diverge from that history?

Rely on testimony

The opinions of others can be a source for your paper. Look to authorities, testimonials, statistics, maxims, laws, and precedents. For example, you might read what critics have to say about *Notebook* with regard to Césaire's relationship to his friend Leopold Sedar Senghor, or you might think about what the poem's continued success says about it.

Developing Your Ideas

You've done some preliminary brainstorming. Perhaps you've even completed a discovery draft. The problem sitting before you now is that you have too many ideas and you don't know what to do with them, or the ideas you've come up with don't seem to be adequately academic. What do you try next?

NUTSHELLING

Nutshelling is the simple process of trying to explain the main point of your observations in a few sentences—in a nutshell. When you put your thoughts in a nutshell, you come to see just how those thoughts fit together. You see how each thought is relevant to the others, and what the overall point is. In short, nutshelling helps you transform your observations or information into something meaningful, focused, and coherent. For instance, if we return to the ideas about

Beckett's *Endgame* from the sections on freewriting and writing a discovery draft, we can nutshell the main points:

> The fact that nothing ever seems to happen in *Endgame* isn't a flaw that makes the play boring—it's actually the main point of the play. The characters are basically just waiting around to die, both unwilling and unable to prevent or delay their deaths, or even to take any meaningful action whatsoever. From Beckett's perspective, that is the fundamental condition of all humans.

BROADENING YOUR TOPIC

What happens when you've put your thoughts in a nutshell and they seem too "small"? You may have come up with a topic that's too narrow, too particular to support a sustained conversation.

Suppose your assignment is to write a paper on Tayeb Salih's "The Doum Tree of Wad Hamid." As you read, you notice a repeating pattern in which various government officials come to the village with a plan to help modernize life there, always at the expense of the sacred tree, and you decide this is a good topic to explore further for your paper.

You take notes about three keys parts of the story: the colonial official who wants to cut down the tree because its location is perfect for the water pump he wants to construct; the post-independence civil servant who wants to build a dock for the river steamer right where the tree is located; and the official, now accompanied by soldiers, from the new Sudanese government, who wants to revive the plan to have the steamer stop in the village. You've made a great observation.

Still, though this observation is a promising one, it still isn't "big" enough. Why not? Because it remains an observation, not an argument. You've listed three incidents that illustrate that none of the three government officials are successful, but you haven't said why these scenes are significant. How do you broaden your topic, from observation to idea, so that you feel you have something important to say?

First, try to make connections. Are there other people—besides these three government officials—who come to the village and leave? Are there other references to modern technology and transportation infrastructure? Is modernization an important theme in the story, and if it is, how do these three incidents relate to the way modernization is portrayed in the rest of the story?

Next, consider the other side of the issue. Is there anything in the story that seems to favor modernization? How does the story present the interplay between those incidents and the repeated failures of government officials?

Third, consider the context. There are, of course, at least two contexts to consider: the context of modern technology within the story, and the larger social and historical context in which the story takes place. Within the story, you might look for the context in which modernization or new technology is presented. Who attempts to bring new technologies? Why do they fail? Is modernization always set in direct opposition to valued village traditions? Might the struggle between modernization and tradition serve as an overarching theme for the story? How do the incidents with the government officials fit into that theme?

Outside the text of the story are other contexts. For instance, the storyteller refers to rule by a foreign government and at least two other Sudanese governments. What was happening in Sudan during this time period? How might those events affect its citizens or its literature?

All of these questions might help you broaden your topic so that you can tie your observations to bigger questions and make your paper more substantial and interesting.

NARROWING/FOCUSING YOUR TOPIC

What if your topic seems too big to handle? What do you do then?

Let's continue thinking about the hypothetical paper on Tayeb Salih's "The Doum Tree of Wad Hamid" that we were just discussing. Perhaps after brainstorming and freewriting, you've concluded that the villagers, despite continually expelling the government officials, are actually not in any way opposed to modernization. This observation is a good start, but you should resist the temptation to be satisfied with it. Simply stating that an opposition to new technologies is not the reason for rejecting the government officials' proposals is not enough. What you need to do now is focus your topic so that your observation can be extended to an interesting conclusion. How do you focus your topic?

First, test your claim. Broad statements are probably not always true, even if they hold true most of the time. Therefore, you need to address any parts of the text that might challenge your claim. Can you find evidence that indicates that villagers are, in fact, opposed to modernization or new technologies? If so, how do you account for that evidence while still defending your claim? In this case, the fact that the villagers repeatedly refuse attempts to introduce new technologies might suggest that they are opposed to modernization. But if you can find a reasonable alternative explanation for their actions, then your claim may still be valid and defensible.

Then look for examples. Find parts of the text that support your claim, and then keep looking and find more. These examples will often make up the majority of your paper, so it's important to be thorough. It's also important to be detailed. Specific examples, rather than broad information, will make your topic clearer and will help you present your argument. For instance, when the storyteller speaks about the inevitability of change, how does he portray the village of the future, with its water pump and steamer stopping place? If you can successfully argue that he presents the future in a positive light, then you have an important part of the text that supports your claim.

Finally, consider the context. Just as a consideration of context can help you broaden an idea, it can also help you focus it. What does modernization mean for these villagers in the context of the historical period? Does the historical and political context provide other reasons the villagers might expel the government officials, or other reasons they may wish to protect their tree?

Essentially, you are looking for details that support your specific claim while simultaneously weeding out other parts of the text because they're not important to your argument. If you fail to go through that process, you may end up including extraneous information in your essay, and your instructor will likely tell you that the paper seems disorganized. If you do a good job of narrowing your focus, that won't be a problem.

Thinking Beyond the Page

So far, we've been advising you to consider the formal aspects of the literature you're writing about—the literature as it is on the page. Sometimes, however, you will want to "think beyond the page" and consider questions about how the work was originally composed, its historical context, and so on. For example, ask yourself the following questions:

What do you know about the author? Learn more about the life and career of the author. If you have some sense of his or her other works, you'll have a better understanding of the themes and genres that interest the author.

What is the history of this work's composition? See if you can discover anything about the conditions under which the work was written. You might find multiple manuscript versions with significant differences, and there may be fascinating reasons for the changes from one version to the next. Molière's play *Tartuffe*, for instance, was first performed in 1664 and was almost immediately banned because the archbishop of Paris threatened to excommunicate anyone who performed in the play, watched a performance, or even read it. A revised version in 1667 didn't fare any better. It wasn't until the third version in 1669 that the play was deemed suitable for public consumption. Even in this last incarnation, the play was rather controversial, and the earlier, censored versions serve to emphasize the elements of the play that caused the controversy.

You might also discover that a text was published in a periodical before being sold in book form. This was quite common for poems and short stories, and novels were often first published serially in magazines or journals. If there are significant differences between the periodical publication and the book publication, you might want to investigate what led to those changes. Was there a *Tartuffe*-style controversy? Or perhaps the changes were due to demands of the marketplace?

In any case, examining multiple versions of the same work can potentially provide you with a lot of interesting information that you can use for a paper. The same may also be true of different translations (see the section "Writing about Adaptation" in Chapter 2 in this guide).

What do the critics and scholars say? Reading what others have said about the work before you read it may help you focus your observations. If (for example) a work is particularly well known for its innovative approach to rendering characters' inner lives, you'll want to pay close attention to this aspect of the work as you read it.

Does the work reflect an interesting cultural phenomenon? Sometimes a professor will ask you to read certain literary works because she wants you to examine a cultural phenomenon. Readers of *Tartuffe*, for instance, often fixate on the role of women in the play. Dorine, a lowly housemaid, is perhaps the most levelheaded character in the play, and she often speaks above her station, arguing with the master of the household. This is behavior that could be frowned upon both because she is a servant and because she is a woman. However, because she is so sensible, her actions are portrayed in a positive light. This aspect of Dorine's character, combined with other aspects of the play, can be read as social criticism, providing commentary on the role of women in seventeenth-century France.

If asking these questions leads you to a promising topic but you find that you don't know enough to write about the topic without reading other sources, then you will need to conduct research in order to write your paper. The next chapter provides some guidance on the research process.

4

Researching World Literature

Doing research in a world literature class is in many ways similar to doing research for other classes: you'll visit the library, find books and journals, get a clear sense of the scholarly conversation, and then offer a perspective of your own. One important difference, though, is that when you write about a work of literature, the literary text itself is typically the primary source, with literary criticism (books, journal articles, and so on) serving as secondary sources.

Understanding Primary and Secondary Sources

Primary sources are defined as any text, object, photograph, film, or other medium that is the object of scholarly investigation. A *secondary source*, on the other hand, is a work that analyzes, comments on, or otherwise sheds light on the primary text, historical event, object, or phenomenon in question.

A source can be primary or secondary, depending on the purpose of your research. For instance, you might write a paper in which the primary text is something other than a literary work (e.g., an author's journal). Or you might write a paper in which a secondary source consists of fictional elements (e.g., a scene that was removed from a novel in an early manuscript stage).

For example, say you are writing a paper on Joseph Conrad's *Heart of Darkness*. You might read what other people have written about the novel, such as Chinua Achebe's famous essay, "An Image of Africa: Racism in Conrad's *Heart of Darkness*." In this situation, *Heart of Darkness* is the primary text, and "An Image of Africa" is a secondary text. However, your professor might assign a paper that is mainly about Achebe's essay. In this situation "An Image of Africa" is the primary text, and other sources you find in your research may act as secondary texts. In fact, one of those secondary texts can be *Heart of Darkness*, if you are using it to help you examine the primary text ("An Image of Africa").

Using Sources

Having a strategy for collecting and employing sources is a good idea. No one wants to wander from source to source trying to remember what, precisely, that source argued, or why it mattered in the first place. We therefore offer the following research tips, which we think will help you become a more effective and efficient researcher.

It may seem at first that these steps take time. "Why should I stop to summarize a source when I can simply go back to the original?" you might wonder. However, the strategies outlined here will save you time in the long run. The work you do to digest and classify your sources as you do your research will make the writing process much more focused, much more efficient, and much less painful in the end.

SUMMARIZE YOUR SOURCES

Before attempting to use any source in your paper, make sure you understand it. The best way to do this is to summarize the source. In summarizing, you accomplish a few things. First, summarizing a source requires you to put the argument in your own language. Some of your secondary sources might use language that puzzles you. When you summarize, you are, in a sense, translating an argument into language that you understand and can work with. Summarizing also helps you see whether there's any aspect of the argument that you aren't getting. If you find yourself stumbling as you attempt to summarize, go back to the original source for clarity.

Summarizing also allows you to restate an argument in terms that are relevant to your paper. Most literary criticism that you will encounter is very complex and offers several ideas for consideration. Some of these ideas will be relevant to your topic, while others will not. When you summarize, you can restate the part of the argument that seems most relevant to the paper you want to write.

Summarizing can also help you organize your source material. If you've used ten sources in a research project, you've probably taken a lot of notes and have gathered several quotations for your paper. This work can amount to pages and pages of text. Summaries can help you organize these notes by telling you almost at a glance which idea comes from which source. You can also include in your summaries a few of the best quotations from each source.

Finally, summarizing is helpful to the entire research process. It's not something that you should do once at the beginning of the research process and then forget about. Every time your understanding of the topic shifts or evolves, take the time to write a brief summary. You'll find that putting your thoughts into writing helps you solidify one stage of understanding before progressing to the next.

CATEGORIZE YOUR SOURCES

Once you've summarized your sources, try to place them into various categories. Remember, writing an academic essay is like taking part in a large, ongoing conversation. Although everyone has a particular point of view, it's safe to say that no one is entering the conversation as a lone wolf. Everyone is speaking from a certain critical perspective. These perspectives might be classified into different groups.

Categorizing your sources might be as simple as looking for similarities among them. Which sources seem to share a point of view? Which seem to arrive at similar conclusions? You will also discover differences among your sources. Try to define these differences and see if they seem to fall into different categories. For example, side A seems to believe X, while side B seems to believe Y. Or, side A attempts to understand the literary work from a feminist perspective, while side B is interested in interpreting the work from a socioeconomic perspective.

Once you've categorized your sources, try to understand what these differences and similarities mean to your argument. Are these categories relevant to the issues you intend to discuss? Where does your own argument fit in? Does the reader need to know about these categories for your argument to make sense? Try to articulate these matters clearly. Write a summary of what you think at this point.

INTERROGATE YOUR SOURCES

In most of the papers that you'll write in college, you'll have to do more than review what other people have said about a topic. You will be asked to present your own point of view. To do this, you'll need to interrogate your sources.

Interrogating your sources does not mean that you have to be contentious. You don't have to search like a bloodhound for the weak spot in an argument. You're not required to "take on" your source. Instead, you'll want to ask questions of your sources. Initiate a conversation: challenge, interrogate, rebut, and confirm. Some good questions to ask are the following:

Is the writer offering evidence for her claims? Is this evidence sufficient? Why or why not?

Is there something that the writer is overlooking? Omitting? If so, is the omission a matter of carelessness, or does it seem purposeful? Why?

Does the writer's argument seem reasonable? If not, can you locate places where the reasoning seems to break down? Can you locate and identify any logical fallacies?

Is the writer's language appropriate? Does she sometimes rely on a pretty phrase or a passionate claim to cover up a lack of evidence?

What can you determine about the writer's perspective? Does she seem to have any important biases? Does she seem to belong to a particular critical school of thought? Does the writer's perspective help or hinder the argument she's trying to make? Why?

Where do you stand in relation to the writer? Do you give her a round of applause? Do you feel like booing her off the stage? Are you sitting with your arms crossed, feeling skeptical?

Keep notes of your personal responses to the writer, and try to translate those responses into comments or questions.

ANNOTATE YOUR SOURCES

Most scholars find it useful whenever possible to mark their texts as they read them. Marking your text enables you to enter into conversations with the author. No longer are you reading passively. Instead, you are reading actively, filling the margins with comments and questions that could blossom into a paper topic down the road. Annotating your texts also ensures that your questions and inspirations won't get lost. Entire books and dissertations have evolved from notes made in the margins. The ideas for these books and dissertations might have been lost had the writer not taken the time to write them down.

You can annotate in various ways. Let's again suppose you are writing a paper on *Heart of Darkness*, and as part of your research you are reading Chinua Achebe's essay "An Image of Africa: Racism in Conrad's *Heart of Darkness*." As Achebe presents each piece of his argument—such as the idea that Conrad is worried about "the lurking hint of kinship"[1] between the Congo and the Thames—you can write in the margin whether you agree with him or not. And, more importantly, you should write why. Perhaps you find a section that you

1 *Massachusetts Review* 18 (1977): 782–794.

believe shows that Achebe's views are biased. This is a key piece of information—underline it, note the bias, and, in the margin, interrogate the bias. It may also be helpful to take quick notes that are purely pragmatic and functional. Where Achebe quotes Conrad, you could write down the page number from your version of *Heart of Darkness* where the quoted passage appears. It will help you cross-reference the text later. Sometimes it may even be helpful to write down any immediate gut reaction you have. In the margin next to the first paragraph of "An Image of Africa," as Achebe relates an incident in which a student told him that "he never had thought of Africa as having [literature and history]," you might write, "Wow, how could a person be this clueless?" Your margin note may not seem especially substantive at first glance, but when you look closer, it's actually a pretty good question: "What is at work in this student's life to perpetuate such a huge error in his worldview?" This question could be the start of an interesting paper.

MAKE YOUR SOURCES WORK FOR YOU

Students often make a grave mistake when they write their first academic papers: overwhelmed by what their sources have to say, they permit their papers to crumble under the weight of scholarly opinion. They end up not writing an informed argument of their own but rehashing what has already been said on a topic. Such a paper might be informative. It might also be competently written. But it does not fulfill the requirements of a good academic paper.

Remember, a good academic paper must be analytical, it must be critical, and it must present a well-crafted, persuasive, informed argument.

Consider the phrase "informed argument." The word with the power in this phrase is the noun "argument." The word "informed" is merely a descriptor. It serves the noun, qualifying it, shading it. The information that you gather should serve your argument in much the same way. Make your sources work for *you*.

You can take some steps to ensure that your sources do indeed work for you without overwhelming your argument. First, don't go to the library or go online before you've thought about your topic on your own. Certainly your research will have an impact on what you think. Sometimes you might even find that you reverse your opinion. But if you go to the library before you've given your topic some thought, you risk jumping on the bandwagon of the first persuasive argument you encounter.

Second, limit your sources to those that are relevant to your topic. It's easy to be swept up in the broader scholarly conversation about your subject and to go off on tangents that don't, in the end, serve your argument.

Finally, keep track of your evolving understanding of the topic by periodically stopping to summarize. As we said earlier, summarizing your sources makes them more manageable.

If you manage your sources as you go along, you will reduce the risk that they'll overwhelm you later.

Keeping Track of Your Sources

During the research process it's very important to keep track of your sources. Nothing is more frustrating than having a great quotation and not knowing where it came from. Develop a good, consistent system for keeping notes.

Every academic discipline requires that you submit with your paper a bibliography or list of works cited. A bibliography should include every work you looked at in your research, even if you didn't quote that source directly. A list of works cited, on the other hand, is just that: a list of works that you quoted, paraphrased, or alluded to in the text of your paper. Both bibliographies and lists of works cited require you to provide information that will make it easier for your reader to find these sources for herself. Consult the MLA (Modern Language Association) Handbook for information about how to construct a proper bibliography and/or list of works cited.

Citing Sources

When you write an academic paper, you must cite all the sources that you've used, even if you don't quote them directly. If you fail to cite these sources, you will be charged with plagiarism. Plagiarism (passing off as your own the words and ideas of others, whether an entire article or just one phrase) is an academic offense for which there are serious consequences.

We can offer several good reasons not to plagiarize. First, it's very easy to get caught. Your instructors—who have spent years teaching students to write and so have read countless student essays—are keenly aware of the difference between professional and student writing. They notice when sophisticated, highly polished academic writing appears out of the blue, with seemingly no development or context. In addition, although the Internet makes plagiarism easy, it also empowers teachers, who can utilize sophisticated search programs to scan literally millions of documents for suspect phrases and sentences.

Second, plagiarism cheats both the reader and the writer. At a fundamental level, citing a source is an academic courtesy. Because scholarship is an ongoing conversation, you should always presume that other students or scholars could want to use your work to develop their own. If you've taken an idea from another scholar but haven't cited it (or have cited it improperly), your reader will have no easy way of finding the source of the ideas that have found their way into your work.

Perhaps the most serious problem raised when you plagiarize or fail to cite your sources is that you're cheating yourself. When you rely on the ideas of others to meet a course requirement, you're denying yourself the opportunity to have the best experience that college can offer: the opportunity to think for yourself. Writing papers can be difficult, and when deadlines loom it can be tempting to look for a shortcut and to lift ideas from scholars who clearly know more about your topic than you do. But it's *your* opinion that your instructor wants to hear. Take each writing assignment as an opportunity to explore and express your ideas. You're paying a lot for this education; you might as well get your money's worth.

5

Developing Your Thesis

Writing a Thesis Sentence

No sentence in your paper will vex you as much as the thesis sentence, and with good reason: the thesis sentence is very often the one sentence in the paper that asserts, controls, and structures the entire argument. Without a strong, persuasive, thoughtful thesis—explicit or implied—a paper might seem unfocused, weak, and not worth the reader's time.

What makes a good thesis sentence? A good thesis sentence generally has the following characteristics:

A good thesis sentence makes a claim. This doesn't mean that you have to reduce an idea to an either-or proposition and then take a stand. Rather, you need to develop an interesting perspective that you can support and defend. This perspective must be more than an observation. "Learning to read and write is important for Frederick Douglass" is merely an observation. Douglass himself comments on that fact on several occasions in his *Narrative*. "Learning to read and write is the most important factor leading to Douglass's escape from slavery" is an argument. Why? Because it posits a perspective. It makes a claim that engages competing claims. Put another way, a good thesis sentence inspires (rather than silences) other points of view. Someone else might argue that the incident in which Douglass fights Mr. Covey is the most important incident in Douglass's life. Another might point to a third factor. In short, if your thesis is positing something that no one can (or would bother to) argue with, then it's not a very good thesis.

A good thesis sentence determines the scope of the argument. The thesis sentence determines what you're required to say in a paper. It also determines what you cannot say. Every paragraph in your paper exists to support or elaborate on your thesis. Accordingly, if one paragraph you've written seems irrelevant to your thesis, you have three choices: get rid of that paragraph, rewrite the thesis sentence, or work to make the paragraph more clearly relevant. Understand that you don't have a fourth option: you can't simply include the idea without making clear its connection to your thesis. The thesis is like a contract between you and your reader. If you introduce ideas that the reader isn't prepared for or doesn't find relevant, you've violated that contract.

A good thesis sentence provides a structure for the argument. The thesis sentence signals to the reader not only what your argument is but how it will be presented. In other words your thesis sentence should either directly or indirectly suggest the structure of your argument to the reader. Say, for example, that you're going to argue the following idea: "That learning to read and write is the most important factor leading to Douglass's escape from slavery is demonstrated in two incidents: A and B." In this case the reader understands that you're going to cover two important points, and that these points will appear in a certain order. If you suggest a particular ordering principle and then abandon it, the reader could feel irritated and confused.

Alternatives to the Thesis Sentence

Sometimes the purpose of a piece of writing is not to make a claim but to raise questions. Other times a writer wants to leave a matter unresolved, inspiring readers to create their own positions. In these cases the thesis sentence might take other forms: the thesis question or the implied thesis.

As we've said, not every piece of writing sets out to make a claim. If your purpose as a writer is to explore, for instance, the reasons for the initial success of *Don Quixote* (a topic for which you're not prepared to make a claim), your thesis question might read, "What cultural forces conspired to make *Don Quixote* a popular success?"

Note that this question, while provocative, does not offer a sense of the argument's structure. It permits the writer to pursue all ideas, without committing to any. Although this freedom might seem appealing, in fact you will find that the lack of a declarative thesis statement requires more work: you need to tighten your internal structure and your transitions from paragraph to paragraph so that the essay is clear and the reader can easily follow your line of inquiry.

But let's suppose, for the sake of illustration, you want to use the thesis question "What cultural forces conspired to make *Don Quixote* a popular success?" You might start by discussing the Spanish Golden Age, and what society looked like in Habsburg Spain. You might follow up by expanding your discussion to look at international contexts, such as the defeat of the Spanish Armada less than two decades prior to the publication of *Don Quixote* (Part I). That discussion of international contexts might include colonial enterprises in the so-called New World, where Spain had a presence. At some point you'll certainly want to touch on the fact that the first part was popular enough to motivate Cervantes to write Part II.

You can see that there's a lot of material to cover here—perhaps too much. If you don't know where the paper will lead or what your conclusions will be, you might find it difficult to avoid digressing into irrelevant tangents. Therefore, if you're going to use a thesis question, make sure that it's a clearly articulated question and that you can structure a well-ordered investigation in response. If the paper starts to feel unwieldy, you might decide instead to use the question as the beginning of a discovery draft. Your findings in the discovery draft can then lead to a declarative thesis for the essay.

One of the most fascinating things about a thesis sentence is that it is the most important sentence in a paper—even when it's not there.

Some of the best writers never explicitly declare a thesis. In some essays you'll find it difficult to point to a single sentence that declares the argument. Still, the essay is coherent and makes a point. In these cases the writers have used an implied thesis.

Writers use an implied thesis when they want readers to come to their own conclusions about the matter at hand. However, just because the writer doesn't declare the thesis doesn't mean that she is working without one. Good writers will clearly state a thesis—either in their own minds or in their notes for the paper. They may elect not to put the thesis in the paper, but each paragraph, each sentence that they write, is controlled by the thesis all the same.

If you decide to write a paper with an implied thesis, be sure that you have a strong grasp of your argument and its structure. Also be sure that you supply adequate transitions so that the reader can follow your argument with ease.

When you begin writing, you should have a solid, well-articulated thesis. The thesis will tell your readers the purpose of your essay, and as you write it will help guide you.

However, it's also important to keep in mind that the thesis you have when you begin is not set in stone; you can still modify it. Often you'll find that as you write, your thoughts about the issue will evolve, and you'll refine your conclusions. Sometimes it will be necessary to change your thesis to reflect those changes in your thinking. Therefore, when you begin writing, what you really have is a *working thesis*. It can change and adapt and develop as you write the paper. A working thesis doesn't necessarily become a final thesis until the paper is finished.

Turning Your Ideas into a Thesis

Now that we've looked at what you want in a thesis, let's take a moment to look at creating one based on work you've already done. Let's say you've done some brainstorming, a little freewriting, and maybe written a discovery draft, and you've come up with some interesting thoughts. After that, you spent a little time nutshelling, trying to focus your ideas. Now you just need to convert one of those focused ideas into a working thesis.

Composing a working thesis is challenging. After all, the thesis is arguably your paper's most important sentence. It cannot be crafted formulaically but must reflect the complexities of the argument that you are hoping to write. But even while no formula exists for writing a successful thesis, we can offer some advice to get you off on the right foot.

First you'll want to determine what you want to write about. Since you've already created some ideas through brainstorming, freewriting, and other exercises, you should have some options. Let's return to the example about Beckett's *Endgame* that we used in Chapter 3, "Generating Ideas." You'll recall that there were plenty of good observations in the accompanying freewriting and discovery draft exercises: repeated words and phrases, humor (or dark humor), Clov's constant threat to leave, waiting for nothing/waiting to die, the condition of humanity, and so on.

From this list of observations, you'll want to find an observation that interests you. You might choose a single observation from your list and focus on it, or you might look for an idea that ties together two or three of these observations, and focus on that. Whatever you decide, don't try to squeeze everything you've observed into a single essay. To do so would require a book—and you simply don't have time to write a book before the paper is due. Determining which idea or set of ideas you want to work with will enable you to stay focused and to do justice to your ideas in the limited time that you have.

Sometimes writers are torn between two or three very good observations. If the ideas can't be synthesized into a single idea or claim, the best strategy is to pick whichever observation looks most interesting. In other words, choose the observation you can have the most fun with. For the sake of this discussion, let's say you decide to write about the repetition you've noticed in *Endgame*. This is a promising topic that offers a lot to talk about—the painkillers, Clov threatening to leave, and so on. It's also a topic that will help you stay focused: you now know not only what you'll want to discuss but what you can leave alone.

You'll also notice something interesting at this point: even though you don't yet have a thesis, the observation you've chosen to write about will help dictate which type of paper you're writing. In this case, since you're writing primarily about repeated words and phrases, you're obviously going to write a textual analysis paper. Again, you now have a strategy that helps you understand not only what you're going to do but what you're not going to do: papers about context, comparison, or adaptation won't really work here.

So now you have your plan: you're going to write a textual analysis paper about repeated words and phrases in Samuel Beckett's *Endgame*. As we noted earlier in this guide, your goal in writing a textual analysis paper is to choose a small textual element and examine in detail how that element contributes to the major themes, underlying message, or overall effect of the text. At this point you need to compose a question, using this goal to guide you. After some doodling you come up with this question: How does Beckett's use of repetition contribute to the overall effect of *Endgame*? Give yourself the opportunity to explore that question. Brainstorm or freewrite a response. Then try to shape your response so that you can answer the question in a couple of sentences, then a single sentence. When you can answer that question in one sentence, you'll have your working thesis.

Of course if you were writing a contextual analysis paper, you'd ask yourself a different question, based on the goals of that type of paper. The same is true for an adaptation paper. The strategy is clear: instead of trying to create a thesis out of thin air, pick an element of the literary work that interests you, then ask yourself a relevant question based on the goals of the type of paper you're going to write. When you answer your own question, you'll have a working thesis.

The Thesis Sentence Checklist

In the end you may have spent a good deal of time writing your working thesis and still not know if it's a good one. As we've indicated earlier, a good thesis typically evolves as the writer writes. As you write, you'll want to interrogate your thesis in order to determine how well it's holding up. Some questions to ask yourself follow:

Does the thesis sentence attempt to answer or to explore a challenging intellectual question? If your thesis doesn't challenge you, it likely won't challenge your reader either. If you find yourself bored as you write, or if you are haunted by the sense that you aren't talking about anything important, stop writing. Return to your list of observations. See if you can find some connection between the observations that might raise the intellectual stakes.

Will the point I'm making generate discussion and argument, or will it leave people asking "So what?"? If your thesis doesn't generate discussion, perhaps the point you made is too obvious. Return to your list of observations. Ask of each one, "Why is this important?" The answer to that question should help you refine your thesis.

Is the thesis too vague? Too general? Should you focus on a more specific aspect of the topic? If a thesis is too broad, it's unlikely to hold the reader's interest. Take your more general idea and link it to specific observations about the text. Perhaps in that linkage you'll find the focus for your paper.

Does the thesis deal directly with the topic at hand, or is it a declaration of my personal feelings? Be careful about personal opinions: to make a claim is different from declaring an opinion. An academic paper does the former but eschews the latter.

Does the thesis indicate the direction of my argument? Does it suggest a structure for my paper? If a thesis is well constructed, it will suggest to you and to your reader where the paper is going. Look at your thesis, then look at your outline. Does your thesis reflect or suggest that outline? Can you rewrite the thesis so that the outline/structure is suggested?

Does the introductory paragraph define terms important to my thesis? Don't make your thesis do all the work. Rely on your introduction to help your thesis, especially when it comes to necessary but cumbersome tasks, such as defining terms.

Does the introduction, when writing a research paper, place my thesis within the larger, ongoing scholarly discussion about the topic? Consider again the dinner party metaphor. What do the scholars at the table have to say about the topic? What do you have to say in response to their ideas? Is the relationship between your perspective and theirs clear to the reader? If not, how might it be made clear?

6

Considering Structure and Organization

Once you've figured out what you want to say, you're left with the problem of how to say it. How should you begin the paper? Should you address the opinions of other thinkers? And what should you do with that stubborn contradiction you've uncovered in your own thinking?

Writing papers in college requires you to come up with sophisticated, complex, and even creative ways of structuring your ideas. Accordingly, we can't offer simple formulas that will work for every paper, every time. We can, however, give you some things to think about that will help you as you consider how to structure your paper.

Let Your Thesis Direct You

Begin by listening to your thesis. If it's well written, it will tell you which way to go with your paper. Suppose, for example, that in responding to Bertolt Brecht's play *The Good Woman of*

Szechwan, and after researching Brecht's other plays, you have written a thesis that says this:

> While Brecht used his theater to promote Marxist ideology, his primary artistic goal was to create a completely new type of theater audience.

This thesis provides the writer with several clues about how best to structure the paper, and it prepares readers for what they will encounter therein. First, the thesis promises readers that the paper will argue that Brecht was interested in more than ideology. The paper will therefore begin by acknowledging that although the promotion of Marxist values was important to him, it was not his only goal. The rest of the paper will concern the (more important) creation of a completely new theater experience—and, by extension, a new type of theater spectator.

We say that this idea of a new theater audience is more important than ideology not necessarily because Brecht himself said so but because the writer seems to say so in her thesis. Reread the thesis sentence. Note that the emphasis falls on the last clause: "his primary artistic goal was to create a completely new type of theater audience." We know that this clause is the emphatic clause because it's the grammatically independent clause. In other words, of the two clauses, this is the one that can stand alone. We also know it's emphatic because of the author's word choice: the phrase "primary artistic goal" underscores the significance of the idea in the second clause. Either way, the emphasis tells us that we will be given not simply a description of how Brecht's plays propagate Marxist ideology but, rather, a description of how his methods of propagating this ideology were used to create a new theater experience that would in turn create a new audience. We understand all of this because the writer took the time to make sure that the thesis was written emphatically.

Sketching Your Argument

Although your thesis will identify your paper's general direction, it will not necessarily provide you with a plan for how to organize all of your points, large and small. Here it might be helpful to diagram or sketch your argument.

In sketching your argument, the goal is to fill the page with your ideas. Begin by writing your thesis. Put it where your instincts tell you to: at the top of the page, in the center, at the bottom. Around the thesis, cluster the points you want to make. Under each of these points, note the observations you've made and the evidence you'll use. Don't get nervous when your sketch starts to look messy. Use arrows. Draw circles. Take up colored pens. Any of these methods can help you find connections between your ideas that otherwise might go unnoticed. Working from your sketch, try to see the line of reasoning that is evolving.

Sketching is an important step in the writing process because it allows you to explore visually the connections between your ideas. If you outline a paper too early in the process, you risk missing these connections. You might line up your points— A, B, C—without fully understanding why. Sketching your argument helps you see, for example, that points A and C really overlap and need to be thought through more carefully.

Outlining Your Argument

When you've finished the sketch, you're ready to make an outline. The task of the outline is to identify the paper's best structure. By "best structure" we mean the structure that best supports the argument you intend to make.

When you're outlining a paper, you'll have many options for organization. Understand, however, that each choice you make eliminates dozens of other options. Your goal is to come up with an outline in which all your choices support your thesis.

Treat the outline as if it were a puzzle that you are putting together. In a puzzle, each piece has only one appropriate place. The same should be true of your paper. If it's easy to shift around your ideas—if several of your paragraphs could be switched around and no one would be the wiser—then you haven't yet found the best structure for your paper. Each paragraph should present a single, well-supported idea that is the logical successor to the ideas that preceded it, all of them building inexorably toward your paper's overall point—the thesis. Keep working until your outline fits your ideas like a glove.

When you think you have an outline that works, challenge it. The first outline rarely holds up to a good interrogation. When you start asking questions of your outline, you will begin to see where the plan holds and where it falls apart. Here are some questions you might ask:

Does my thesis control the direction of the outline?

Are all of my main points relevant to the thesis?

Can any of these points be moved around without changing something important about the thesis?

Does the outline seem logical?

Does the argument progress, or does it stall?

If the argument seems to take a turn midstream, does the thesis anticipate that turn?

Do I have sufficient support for each of my points?

Have I made room in the outline for other points of view about the topic?

Does this outline reflect a thorough, thoughtful argument? Have I covered the ground?

Constructing Paragraphs

Imagine that you've written the thesis. You've interrogated the outline. You know which modes of arrangement you intend to use. You've settled on a plan that you think will work. Now you have to go about the serious business of constructing paragraphs.

You were probably told in high school that paragraphs are the workhorses of a paper. Indeed they are. If a single paragraph is incoherent or weak, the entire argument might fail. It's important that you consider carefully the "job" of each paragraph. Know what you want that paragraph to do. Make sure it pulls its weight.

WHAT IS A PARAGRAPH?

A paragraph is generally understood as a single "unit" of a paper. What your readers expect when they encounter a new paragraph is that you're going to declare a point and then offer support for that point. If you violate this expectation—if your paragraphs wander aimlessly among a half dozen points, or if they declare points without offering any evidence to support them—readers will become confused or irritated by your argument. They won't want to read any further.

WHAT SHOULD A PARAGRAPH DO?

At the risk of sounding silly, we suggest that you consider this: what you look for in a boyfriend or girlfriend, a reader looks for in a paragraph. You want a partner who is supportive, strong, and considerate to others. Similarly, a good paragraph is:

- **Supportive.** Even in the most trying of times a good paragraph finds a way to support the thesis. It declares its relationship to the thesis clearly, so that the whole world knows what the paragraph intends to do. In other words, a supportive paragraph's main idea clearly develops the argument of the thesis.
- **Strong.** A good paragraph isn't bloated with irrelevant evidence or redundant sentences. Nor is it a scrawny thing, begging to be fed. It's strong and buff. You know that it's been worked on. In other words, a strong paragraph develops its main idea, using sufficient evidence.
- **Considerate.** Good paragraphs consider their relationship to other paragraphs. A good paragraph never interrupts its fellow paragraphs to babble on about its own irrelevant problems. A good paragraph waits its turn. It shows up when and where it's supposed to. It doesn't make a mess for other paragraphs to clean up. In other words, a considerate paragraph is a coherent paragraph. It makes sense within the text as a whole.

WRITING THE TOPIC SENTENCE
OR GUIDING CLAIM

Just as every paper requires a thesis sentence to assert and control its argument, so also every paragraph requires a topic sentence to assert and control its main idea. Without a topic sentence, your paragraphs will seem jumbled, aimless. Your reader will become confused. Because the topic sentence plays an important role in your paragraph, it must be crafted with care. When you've written a topic sentence, ask yourself the following questions:

Does the topic sentence declare a single point of the argument? Because the reader expects that a paragraph will explore only one idea in your paper, it's important that your topic sentence not be too ambitious. If it points to two or three ideas, perhaps you need to consider developing more paragraphs.

Does the topic sentence further the argument? Give your topic sentences the same "so what?" test that you gave your thesis sentence. If your topic sentence isn't interesting, your paragraph probably won't further the argument. Your paper could stall.

Is the topic sentence relevant to the thesis? It might seem so to you, but the relevance may not be so clear to your reader. If you find that your topic sentence is taking you into brand-new territory, stop writing and consider your options.

If the new territory isn't relevant to the existing thesis, either you'll have to rewrite your thesis to accommodate this new direction, or you'll have to consider excluding this paragraph from your final paper.

Is there a clear relationship between this topic sentence and the paragraph that came before? Make sure that you haven't left out any steps in the process of composing your argument. If you take a sudden turn in your reasoning, signify that turn to the reader by using the proper transitional phrase—"on the other hand," "however," or the like.

Does the topic sentence control the paragraph? If your paragraph seems to unravel, take a second look. Perhaps the topic sentence isn't adequately controlling the paragraph and needs to be rewritten. Or, maybe the paragraph is moving on to a new idea that needs to be developed in a paragraph of its own.

Where have I placed my topic sentence? Readers often look for topic sentences at or near the beginning of a paragraph. Consider this: If you are skimming something quickly, which sentence do you look to in each paragraph? Likely it's the first sentence. But that doesn't mean all of your topic sentences need to be situated at the beginning of your paragraphs. Nevertheless, if you're going to place your topic sentence elsewhere, you'll need to craft your paragraph with care. You might justify putting the topic sentence in the middle of the paragraph, for example, if you have information that needs to precede it. You might also justify putting the topic sentence at the end of the paragraph, if you want the reader to consider your line of reasoning before you declare your main point. Let the argument and what it needs dictate where you place your topic sentence. Wherever you place it, be strategic. Make sure that your decision facilitates your argument.

Developing Your Paragraphs

EVIDENCE

Students often ask how long a paragraph should be. To this we respond, "As long as it takes."

It's possible to make a point quickly. Sometimes it's desirable to keep it short. Notice the preceding paragraph, for example. We might have hemmed and hawed, talked about short paragraphs and long paragraphs. We might have said that the average paragraph is one-half to two-thirds of a page in length. We might have spent time explaining why the too-short paragraph is too short, and the too-long paragraph too long. Instead, we cut to the chase. After huffing and puffing through this paragraph (which is getting longer and longer all the time), we'll give you the same advice: a good paragraph is as long as it needs to be in order to illustrate, explore, and/or prove its main idea.

However, length isn't all that matters in paragraph development. What's important is that a paragraph develops its idea fully, and in a manner that readers can follow with ease.

Let's consider these two issues carefully. First, how do we know when an idea is fully developed? If your topic sentence is well written, it should tell you what the paragraph needs to do. If the topic sentence declares, for example, that there are two conflicting impulses at work in a particular fictional character, then the reader will expect the two impulses to be defined and illustrated. It might take two paragraphs to do this; it might take one. The decision will depend on how important this matter is to the discussion. If the point is important, you'll take your time, and (more likely than not) you'll use at least two paragraphs. In this case a topic sentence might be understood as controlling not only a paragraph but an entire section of text.

When you've written a paragraph, ask yourself the following questions:

Do I have enough evidence to support this paragraph's idea?

Do I have too much evidence? In other words, will the reader be lost in a morass of details, unable to see the argument as a whole?

Does this evidence clearly support the assertion that I'm making in this paragraph, or am I stretching it?

If I'm stretching it, what can I do to persuade the reader that this stretch is worth making?

Am I repeating myself in this paragraph?

Have I defined all of the paragraph's important terms?

Can I say, in a nutshell, what the purpose of this paragraph is? Has the paragraph fulfilled that purpose?

ARRANGEMENT

Equally important to the idea of a paragraph's development is the matter of the paragraph's arrangement. Paragraphs are arranged differently for different purposes. For example, if you're writing a paper about an oral epic's history and wish to summarize a sequence of events, you'll likely want to arrange the information chronologically. If you're writing a paper in which you want to describe the appearance of slave narratives in different cultures during roughly the same time, perhaps you'll choose to arrange the information spatially. You could start with African American narratives, followed by West African narratives, followed by Caribbean narratives. If you're writing a paper about the elements of a novel that make it stand out from other novels of a similar type, you might want to arrange your ideas by working from the specific to the general—and so on.

COHERENCE

So you have your thesis, your topic sentences, and truckloads of evidence to support the whole lot. You've spent three days writing your paragraphs, making sure that each paragraph argues one point and that this point is well supported with textual evidence. But when you read the essay back to yourself, you feel a profound sense of disappointment. Though you've followed your outline, the essay just doesn't seem to hold together. It could be that you have a problem with coherence.

A lack of coherence is easy to diagnose but not so easy to cure. An incoherent essay doesn't seem to flow. Its arguments are hard to understand. The reader has to double back again and again in order to follow the gist of the argument. Something has gone wrong. What?

Look for the following issues in your paper:

Make sure the grammatical subjects of your sentences reflect the real subject of your paragraph. Underline the subjects of all the sentences in the paragraph. Do these subjects match the paragraph's subject in most cases? Or, have you put the paragraph's subject into another, less important part of the sentence? Remember that the reader understands an idea's importance according to where you place it. If your main idea is hidden as an object of a preposition in a subordinate clause, do you really think your reader is going to follow what you're trying to say? For instance, consider the following paragraph about the way Frederick Douglass discusses religion in *The Narrative of the Life of Frederick Douglass*. The grammatical subject of each sentence is underlined.

Many situations occur throughout Douglass's *Narrative* in which Douglass witnesses slaveholders using the Bible to justify their actions. An excellent example is Master Thomas's conversion. Beforehand, Thomas had "relied upon his own depravity to shield and sustain him in his savage barbarity, but after his conversion, he found religious sanction and support for his slaveholding cruelty." This idea appears most clearly when he whips a woman while quoting scripture: "He that knoweth his master's will, and doeth it not, shall be beaten with many stripes."

Look at the four subjects: "situations," "example," "Thomas," and "idea." Of these, only "Thomas" is clearly related to the topic of the paragraph. Now consider this revised paragraph:

Throughout his *Narrative*, Douglass offers several instances of slaveholders who use the Bible to justify their actions. He recounts in particular the story of Master Thomas, who "relied upon his own depravity to shield and sustain him in his savage barbarity, but who, after his conversion . . . found religious sanction and support for his slaveholding cruelty." Douglass elaborates by relating an incident in which Master Thomas, while whipping a naked woman with a heavy cow skin, justifies his actions by quoting scripture: "He that knoweth his master's will, and doeth it not, shall be beaten with many stripes."

Look at the subjects here. All refer to "Douglass." The paragraph's similar string of subjects keeps the reader focused on the topic and creates a paragraph that flows more naturally and seems much more coherent than the first one.

Make sure the grammatical subjects are consistent. Again, look at the grammatical subjects of all your sentences. How many different subjects do you find? If you have too many different sentence subjects, your paragraph will be hard to follow.

Make sure your sentences look backward as well as forward. For a paragraph to be coherent, each sentence should begin by linking itself firmly to the sentence that preceded it. If the link between sentences does not seem firm, use an introductory clause or phrase to connect one idea to the other.

Follow the principle of moving from old to new. If you put the old information at the beginning of the sentence and the new information at the end, you accomplish two things: first, you ensure that your readers are on solid ground, moving from the familiar to the unknown, and, second, because we tend to give emphasis to what comes at the end of a sentence, readers rightfully perceive that the new information is more important than the old.

Use repetition to create a sense of unity. Repeating key words and phrases at appropriate moments will give your readers a sense of coherence in your work. But don't overdo it; you'll risk sounding redundant.

Use transition markers wisely. Sometimes you'll need to announce to your readers a turn in your argument, or you'll want to emphasize one point, or you'll want to make clear a particular relationship in time. In all these cases you'll want to use transition markers. Some examples follow:

- **To give an example:** *for example, for instance*
- **To present a list:** *first, second, third, next, then*
- **To show that you have more to say:** *in addition, furthermore, moreover*
- **To indicate similarity:** *also, likewise, similarly*
- **To show an exception:** *but, however, nevertheless, on the other hand*
- **To show cause and effect:** *accordingly, consequently, therefore, because*
- **To emphasize:** *indeed, in fact, of course*
- **To conclude:** *finally, in conclusion, in the end*

Introductions and Conclusions

Introductions and conclusions are among the most challenging of all paragraphs. Why? Because they must do more than state a topic sentence and offer support. Introductions and conclusions must synthesize and provide context for your entire argument, and they must also make the proper impression on your readers.

The introduction is your chance to get readers interested in your subject. Accordingly, the tone of the paragraph has to be just right. You want to inform, but not to the point of being dull; you want to intrigue, but not to the point of being vague; you want to take a strong stance, but not to the point of alienating readers. Pay attention to the nuances of your tone. Seek out a second reader if you're not sure that you've managed to get the tone the way you want it.

Equally important to the tone of the introduction is that it needs to "place" your argument into a larger context. Some strategies follow:

Announce your topic broadly; then declare your particular take. For example, if you're interested in talking about the symbolism in Henrik Ibsen's *Hedda Gabler*, you might (1) begin by saying that Ibsen's symbolism has posed a problem for many of his critics, (2) provide a quick definition of the problem as others have defined it, and (3) declare your thesis (which states your own position on the matter).

Provide any background material important to your argument. If you're interested in exploring how writers of the modernist movement influenced the work of Samuel Beckett, in your introduction you'll want to provide, in broad strokes, a description of modernism. Don't include irrelevant details in your description; instead, emphasize those aspects of the movement that might have most influenced Beckett.

Define key terms as you intend to make use of them in your argument. If, for example, you're writing a paper on Noh, it is absolutely essential that you define the term for your reader. Begin with a definition of terms, and from there work toward the declaration of your argument.

Use an anecdote or a quotation. Sometimes you'll find a terrific story or quotation that seems to reflect the main point of your paper. Don't be afraid to begin with it. Be sure, however, that you tie that story or quotation clearly and immediately to your main argument.

Acknowledge your opponents. When you're writing a paper about a controversial matter, you might wish to begin by summarizing the point of view of your adversaries. Then state your own position in opposition to theirs. In this way you place yourself clearly in the ongoing conversation.

Remember, the introduction is the first impression that your argument will make on the reader. Take special care with your sentences so that they'll be interesting. Also take the time to consider who your readers are and what background they will bring with them to their reading. If your readers are very knowledgeable about the subject, you will not need to provide a lot of background information. If your readers are less knowledgeable, you will need to be more careful about defining terms.

Finally, you might want to consider writing the introduction after you've written the rest of the paper. Many writers find that they have a better grip on their subject once they've done a first draft. This "better grip" helps them craft an introduction that is sure-footed, persuasive, interesting, and clear. But be careful. Any changes that you make to an introduction and/or a thesis statement will affect the paper that follows. Simply adding the new introductory paragraph will not produce a "completed" paper.

Conclusions are also difficult to write. How do you manage to make the reader feel persuaded by what you've said? Even if the points of your paper are strong, the overall effect of your argument might fall to pieces if the paper as a whole is badly concluded.

Many students end their papers by simply summarizing what has come before. A summary of what the reader has just read is important to the conclusion—particularly if your argument has been complicated or has covered a lot of ground. But a good conclusion will do more. Just as the introduction sought to place the paper in the larger, ongoing conversation about the topic, so should the conclusion insist on returning readers to that ongoing conversation, but with the feeling that they've learned something more. You don't want readers to finish your paper and say "So what?" Admittedly, writing a conclusion isn't easy.

Many of the strategies we've listed for improving introductions can help you improve your conclusions as well. In the conclusion you might do the following:

Return to the ongoing conversation, emphasizing the importance of your own contribution to it.

Consider again the background information with which you began, and illustrate how your argument has shed new light on that information.

Return to the key terms and point out how your essay has added new dimension to their meanings.

Use an anecdote or a quotation that summarizes or reflects your main idea.

Acknowledge your opponents—if only to emphasize that you've countered their positions successfully.

Remember, language is especially important to a conclusion. Your goal in the final sentences is to leave your ideas resounding in the reader's mind. Give the reader something to think about. Make your language ring.

7

Attending to Style

Most of us know good style when we see it—and *hear* it in the mind's ear. We also know when a sentence seems cumbersome to read. However, though we can easily spot beastly sentences, it is not as easy to say why a sentence—especially one that is grammatically correct—isn't working. We look at the sentence; we see that the commas are in the right places; and we find no error to speak of. So why is the sentence so awful? What's gone wrong?

When thinking about what makes a good sentence, be sure to put yourself in the reader's place. What is a reader hoping to find in your sentences? Information, yes. Eloquence, surely. But, most important, a reader is looking for clarity. Your reader does not want to wrestle with sentences. She wants to read with ease. She wants to see one idea build on another. She wants to experience, without struggling, the emphasis of your language and the importance of your idea. Above all, she wants to feel that you, the writer, are doing the bulk of the work. In short, she wants to read sentences that are persuasive, straightforward, and clear.[2]

Basic Principles of the Sentence

FOCUS ON ACTORS AND ACTIONS

To understand what makes a good sentence, it's important to understand one principle: a sentence, at its very basic level, is about actors and actions. As such, the subject of a sentence should point clearly to the actor, and the verb of the sentence should describe the important action.

This principle might seem so obvious to you that you don't think it warrants further discussion. But think again. Look at the following sentence, and then try to determine, in a nutshell, what's wrong with it:

> There is a question in the mind of some critics over whether the employment of extensive dialogue is a sign of weakness in a novel.

This sentence has no grammatical errors. But certainly it lumbers along, without any force. What are the actors? What are the actions?

---

2 The way of teaching style that is represented here has been greatly influenced by Joseph Williams and his work. For a thorough examination of the fundamental principles of style, see Williams's *Style: Lessons in Clarity and Grace*, 10th ed. (New York: Pearson Longman, 2010).

Now consider the following sentence:

Some critics question whether extensive dialogue signi-
fies a weak novel.

What changes does this sentence make? We can point to the
more obvious changes: omitting the empty *there is* phrase;
replacing the abstract noun *sign* with the stronger verb *signify*;
replacing a second abstract noun *weakness* with the adjective
weak; omitting all of the prepositions that the abstract nouns
require. What principle governs these many changes? Precisely the one mentioned earlier: that the *actors* in a sentence should serve as the sentence's grammatical subjects,
and the *actions* should be illustrated forcefully in the sentence's
verbs.

Whenever you feel that your prose is confusing or hard to
follow, find the actors and the actions of your sentences. Is the
actor the subject of your sentence? Is the action related, viv-
idly, in a verb? If not, rewrite your sentences accordingly.

BE CONCRETE

Student writers tend to rely too heavily on abstract nouns:
they use *expectation* when the verb *expect* is stronger; they
write *evaluation* when *evaluate* is more vivid. So why use an
abstract noun when a verb will do better? Many students
believe that abstract nouns permit them to sound more "academic." When you write with a lot of abstract nouns, however,

you risk confusing your reader. You also end up cornering yourself syntactically. Consider the following:

Nouns often require prepositions. Too many prepositional phrases in a sentence are hard to follow. Verbs, on the other hand, can stand on their own. They're cleaner; they don't box you in. If you need some proof of this claim, consider the following sentence:

> Oral performances of the work by griots occurred long before the work was put into writing by poets.

Notice all of the prepositional phrases that these nouns require. Now look at the following sentence, which uses verbs:

> Griots performed the work long before poets wrote it down.

This sentence has fewer nouns and prepositions and is therefore much easier to read—yet it still conveys all the information found in the prior sentence.

Abstract nouns often invite the *there is* construction. Consider the following sentence:

> There is a method of narration that James Joyce pioneered called "stream of consciousness" in which the inner

thoughts of characters are rendered in dissociated and convoluted form.

We might rewrite this sentence as follows:

James Joyce pioneered a method of narration called "stream of consciousness" that renders characters' thoughts in dissociated and convoluted form.

The result, again, is a sentence that is more direct and easier to read.

Abstract nouns are, well, abstract. Using too many abstract nouns will leave your prose seeming ungrounded. Words such as *falsification, beauteousness,* and *insubstantiality* sound pompous and vague—which may be exactly what you want, if you're striving for a slightly comic, self-mocking effect. But, by and large, people simply don't talk this way. Instead, use concrete nouns, as well as strong verbs, to convey your ideas. *Lying, beauty,* and *flimsiness* reflect the way people really speak; these words point directly to their meanings without drawing undue attention to themselves.

Abstract nouns can obscure your logic. Note how hard it is to follow the line of reasoning in the following sentence (the nouns that might be rewritten as verbs or as adjectives are in boldface):

Decisions with regard to **the elimination** of characters from a novel on the basis of **their insignificance** to the developing narrative rest with the author.

Now consider this sentence:

When characters are no longer significant to a narrative, the author can decide to eliminate them from his novel.

The Exception: When to Use Abstract Nouns

In some instances an abstract noun will be essential to the sentence. Sometimes abstract nouns refer to a previous sentence (*these arguments, this decision,* etc.). Other times they allow you to be more concise (e.g., *her argument* versus *what she argued*). And, in other cases, the abstract noun is a concept important to your argument: freedom, love, revolution, and so on. Still, if you examine your prose, you'll probably find that you overuse abstract nouns. Omitting from your writing those abstract nouns that aren't really necessary makes for leaner, "fitter" prose.

BE CONCISE

One of the most exasperating aspects of reading student texts is that most students don't know how to write concisely. Students use phrases when a single word will do, offer pairs of adjectives and verbs where one is enough, or overwrite, saying the same thing two or three times with the hope that the reader will be impressed by a point worth rephrasing and then rephrasing again.

Stop the madness! It's easy to delete words and phrases from your prose once you've learned to be ruthless about it.

Do you really need words such as *actually, basically, generally*, and so on? If you don't need them, why are they there? Are you using two words where one will do? Isn't the phrase *first and foremost* redundant? What's the point of *future* in *future plans*? And why do you keep saying, *"In my opinion"*? Doesn't the reader understand that this is your paper, based on your point of view? Does drawing attention to yourself in this way make your points any stronger—or does it have the opposite effect, coming across as insecurity or as hedging?

Sometimes you won't be able to fix a wordy sentence by simply deleting a few words or phrases. You'll have to rewrite the whole sentence. Take the following sentence, for example:

> Plagiarism is a serious academic offense resulting in punishments that might include suspension or dismissal, profoundly affecting your academic career.

The idea here is simple: *Plagiarism is a serious offense with serious consequences.* Why not simply say so? Don't be afraid to let your reader connect your ideas to the context—at its most pleasurable, good writing gives the reader a sense of collaboration, of being trusted to connect the dots.

BE COHERENT

At this point in discussing style, we move from the sentence as a discrete unit to the way that sentences fit together. Coherence (or the lack of it) is a common problem in student papers. Sometimes a professor encounters a paper in which all the ideas seem to be there, but they're hard to follow. The prose seems jumbled. The line of reasoning is anything but linear. Couldn't the student have made this paper a bit more readable?

Although coherence is a complicated and difficult matter to address, we can offer a couple of tricks that will help your sentences "flow." Silly as it sounds, you should "dress" your sentences the way a bride might—wear, as the saying goes, something old and something new. In other words most of the sentences you write should begin with the old—with something that looks back to the previous sentence. Then your sentence should move on to telling the reader something new. If you do this, your line of reasoning will be easier for readers to follow.

Though this advice sounds simple enough, it is not always easy to follow. Let's dissect the practice so that we can better understand how our sentences might be "well dressed."

Consider, first, the beginnings of sentences. The coherence of your paper depends largely on how well you begin sentences. "Well begun is half done" says Mary Poppins, and in this case (as in all cases, really) she's right.

Beginning a sentence is hard work. When you begin a sentence, you have three important matters to consider:

1. **Is your topic also the subject of the sentence?** When a sentence lacks coherence, usually it's because the writer has not been careful to ensure that the topic of the sentence is also the grammatical subject of the sentence. If, for instance, you're writing a paper about Zeami's Noh drama *Atsumori*, and at one point you include a sentence whose topic is the importance of traditional Noh masks in staging the play, then the grammatical subject of the sentence should reflect that idea:

> **The actors' masks** are a crucial element of any performance of *Atsumori*; they are just as important as the dialogue.

If, on the other hand, you bury your topic in a subordinate clause, look what happens:

> *An important part of performing* Atsumori *is the staging, such as* **the use of masks for the actors,** *which is just as important as the actors' dialogue.*

The emphasis and focus of the sentence are obscured.

2. **Are the topics/subjects of your sentences consistent?** For a paragraph to be coherent, most of the sentence subjects should be the same. To check for consistency, pick out a paragraph and make a list of its sentence subjects. See if any of the subjects seem out of place. For example, suppose

you're writing a paragraph comparing ancient Greek drama, Japanese Noh drama, and Indian classical drama (such as *Sakuntala and the Ring of Recollection*) in terms of their intended effect on audiences. Do most of your sentence subjects reflect that paragraph topic? Or, do some of your sentences have other, tangential topics as the grammatical subject? Although the full extent of the influence of this topic may indeed have a place in your paper, you will confuse readers if your paragraph's sentence subjects point to too many competing ideas. Revise the sentences (perhaps the entire paragraph) for coherence.

3. **Have you marked, when appropriate, the transitions between ideas?** Coherence depends on how well you connect a sentence to the one that came before it. You'll want to make solid transitions between your sentences, using words such as *however* or *therefore*. You'll also want to signal to readers whenever, for example, something important or disappointing comes up. In these cases you'll want to use expressions such as *note that* or *unfortunately*. You might also want to indicate time or place in your argument. If so, you'll use transitions such as *then, later, earlier*, or *in the previous paragraph*. Be careful not to overuse transition phrases. Some writers think transition phrases can, all by themselves, direct a reader through an argument. Indeed, sometimes all a paragraph needs is a *however* in order for its argument suddenly to make sense. More often, though,

the problem with coherence does not stem from a lack of transition phrases but from the fact that the writer has not articulated, for himself, the connections between his ideas. Don't rely on transition phrases alone to bring sense to muddled prose.

BE EMPHATIC

We've been talking about how sentences begin, but what about how they end?

If the beginnings of sentences must look over their shoulders at what came before, the ends of sentences must forge ahead into new ground. It's the end of a sentence, then, that must be courageous and emphatic. You must construct sentences so that the ends pack the punch.

To write emphatically, follow these principles:

Declare important ideas at the end of a sentence. Shift less important ideas to the front.

Tighten the ends of sentences. Don't trail off into nonsense, don't repeat yourself, and don't qualify what you've just said if you don't have to. Simply make your point and move on.

Use subordinate clauses to house subordinate ideas. Put all the important ideas in main clauses and the less important ideas in subordinate clauses. If you have two ideas of equal importance that you want to express in the same sentence, use parallel constructions or semicolons. These two tricks of the trade are perhaps more useful than any others in balancing equally significant ideas.

BE IN CONTROL

When sentences run on and on, readers know that a writer has lost control. Take command of your sentences. When you read over your paper, look for sentences that never seem to end. Your first impulse might be to take these long sentences and divide them into two (or three or four). This simple solution often works. But sometimes this strategy isn't the most desirable one; it might lead to short, choppy sentences. Moreover, if you always cut your sentences in two, you'll never learn how a sentence can be long and complex without violating the boundaries of good prose.

What do you do when you encounter an overly long sentence? First consider the point of your sentence. Usually it will have more than one point, and sorting out the points helps sort out the grammar. Consider carefully the points that you're trying to make and the connections between those points. Then try to determine which grammatical structure best serves your purpose.

Are the points of equal importance? Use a coordinating conjunction (*and, but, or*) or a semicolon to join the ideas. Try to use parallel constructions when appropriate.

Are the points of unequal importance? Use subordinate clauses (*although, while, because,* and so on) or relative clauses (*that, which*) to join the ideas, putting the less important idea in the subordinate clause.

Does one point make for an interesting aside? Insert that point between commas, dashes, or even parentheses at the appropriate juncture in the sentence.

Do these ideas belong in the same sentence? If not, create two sentences.

WRITE BEAUTIFULLY

In your career as a writer you will sometimes produce a paper that is well written but could be written better. On this happy occasion, you might wish to turn your attention to such matters as balance, parallel structure, emphasis, rhythm, and word choice. If you're interested in exploring these rhetorical tools, consult one of several excellent style books, such as Joe Williams's *Style: The Basics of Clarity and Grace,* William Strunk Jr. and E. B. White's *The Elements of Style,* or John Trimble's *Writing with Style.* You will find plenty of valuable advice in any one of these sources.

8

Revising Your Work

Why and How to Revise

Most of us who compose on a computer understand revision as an ongoing—even constant—process. Every time you hit the delete key, every time you cut and paste, and every time you take out a comma or exchange one word for another, you're revising.

Real revision, however, is more than making a few changes here and there. Real revision, just as the word implies, calls for *seeing again*; it requires that you open yourself up to the possibility that parts of your paper—even your entire paper— might need to be rethought, and rewritten.

Achieving this state of mind is difficult. First, you might be very attached to what you've written. You might be unwilling to change a word, let alone three or four paragraphs. Second, there's the matter of time: you might sense that the paper needs major work, but it's due tomorrow, or you have an exam in physics, or you're coming down with a cold and know that you need to sleep. Third, you might have difficulty understanding what, exactly, is wrong with your paper. Finally, you might simply be sick and tired of the paper. How can you make another pass through it when exhaustion has you in its grip? Why should you be bothered with (or let yourself be over-whelmed by) the process of revising?

Of course we might convince you that revision is worth the extra effort simply by saying that revising a paper will help you achieve a better grade. A good reader can sense when a piece of writing has been thoroughly considered and recon-sidered. This consideration (and here we mean the word in both of its meanings) is not lost on your professor and will be rewarded.

More important than grades, however, is the fact that revising your papers teaches you to be a better writer. Profes-sional writers know that to write is to rewrite. In the revision process you improve your reading skills and your analytical skills. You learn to challenge your own ideas, thus deepen-ing and strengthening your argument. You learn to find the weaknesses in your writing. You may even discover patterns of error or habits of organization that are undermining your papers.

Though revising takes time and energy, it also will help you become a more efficient writer down the road. If, for example, you have discovered through the revision process that you tend to bury your topic sentences in the middle of your paragraphs, you can take this discovery with you as you draft your next paper. You may then be less likely to make that particular mistake again.

Perhaps we've answered the question "Why should I revise?" The next question, of course, is "How?" There are many different kinds of revising, including the following:

Large-scale revision. Large-scale revision means looking at the entire paper for places where your thinking seems to go awry. You might need to provide evidence, define terms, or add an entirely new step to your reasoning. You might even decide to restructure or rewrite your paper completely if you discover a new idea that intrigues you, or a structure that seems to be more effective than the one you've been using.

Small-scale revision. Small-scale revision needs to happen when you know that a certain part of your paper isn't working. Maybe the introduction needs work. Maybe one part of the argument seems weak. Once you've located the problem, you'll focus on revising that one section of your paper. When you're finished you'll want to reconsider your paper as a whole to make sure that your revisions work in the context of the entire paper.

Editing. Too often students confuse editing with revision. They are not the same processes. Editing is the process of finding minor problems with a text—problems that might easily be fixed by deleting a word or sentence, cutting and pasting a paragraph, and so on. When you edit, you're considering your reader. You might be happy with how you've written your paper, but will your reader find your paper clear, readable, and interesting? How can you rewrite the paper so that it's clearer, more concise, and, most important of all, a pleasure to read?

The very best writers revise their writing in all the ways listed here. To manage these various levels of revision, it's very important that you get an early start on your papers so that you have time to make any substantive, large-scale revisions that might be needed. Good writers also understand that revision is an ongoing process, not necessarily something that you do only after your first draft is complete. You might find, for example, that you're stuck halfway through the first draft of your paper. You decide to take a look at what you have so far. As you read, you find that you've neglected to make a point that is essential to the success of your argument. You revise what you've written, making that point clear. In the end you find that your block, your "stuckness," is gone. Why? Maybe it's gone because what was blocking you in the first place was a hole in your argument. Or, maybe it's gone because you gave your brain a break. In any case, stopping to revise in the middle of the drafting process often proves wise.

Developing a Critical Eye

We have yet to address the matter of how a writer knows what she should revise. Developing a critical eye is perhaps the most difficult part of the revision process. But having a critical eye makes you a better writer, reader, and thinker. So it's worth considering carefully how you might learn to see your own work with the objectivity that is essential to successful self-criticism.

The first step in developing a critical eye is to get some distance from your work. If you've planned your writing process well, you'll have left yourself a day or two to take a break. If you don't have this luxury, even an hour of video games or a walk over to the printing center to pick up a hard copy of your draft might be enough to clear your head. Many writers find that their mind keeps working on their papers even while their attention is turned elsewhere. When they return to their work, they bring with them a fresh perspective. They also bring a more open mind.

When you return to your paper, the first thing you'll want to do is consider whether or not the paper as a whole meets your (and your professor's) expectations. Read the paper through without stopping (don't get hung up on one troublesome paragraph). Then ask yourself the following questions:

Did I fulfill the assignment? If the professor gave you instructions for this assignment, reread them and then ask yourself whether or not you've addressed all of the matters you're expected to address. Does your paper stray from the assignment? If it does, have you worked to make your argument relevant, or are you coming out of left field? If the professor hasn't given you explicit instructions for this paper, you'll still want to take a moment to consider what she or he expects. What books has the professor asked you to read? What position does he or she take toward your topic? Has the professor emphasized a certain method of scholarship (feminism, Marxism, etc.)? Has she or he said anything to you about research methods in his or her discipline? Does your paper seem to fit into the conversation that the professor has been carrying on in class? Have you written something that other students would find relevant and interesting?

Did I say what I intended to say? This question is perhaps the most difficult question you will ask yourself in the revision process. Many of us think that we have indeed said what we intended to say. When we read our papers, we're able to fill in any holes that might exist in our arguments with the information that we have in our minds. The problem is that our readers sometimes don't have this same information in mind. Your challenge in revising your own writing, therefore, is to forget about what you *meant* and see only what you actually *wrote*—the meaning has to be right there in the words on the page. It's very important to think carefully about what you've said—and to think just as carefully about what you haven't said. Ask yourself the following questions: Was I clear? Do I need to define my terms? Has every stage of the argument been articulated clearly? Have I made adequate transitions between my ideas? Is my logic solid—is it there for all to see? If the answer to any of these questions is no, you will want to revise your draft.

What are the strengths of my paper? In order to develop a critical eye it's just as important to know when you've written well as it is to know when you've written poorly. It helps, therefore, to make a list of what you think you've done well in your draft. It's also helpful to pick out your favorite or strongest paragraph. When you find a good paragraph, sentence, or idea, think about why it's good. You'll not only be gaining an understanding of what it means to write well, but you'll also be giving yourself a pat on the back—something that's very important to do in the revision process.

What are the weaknesses of my paper? Looking for weaknesses isn't as fun as looking for strengths, but it's necessary to the revision process. Again, try to make a list of what you haven't done well in this paper. Your list should be as specific as you can make it. Instead of writing "problems with paragraphs," you might say, "problems with unity in my paragraphs," or, even more specific, "problems with the transitions between paragraphs 3 and 4, and 12 and 13." Also force yourself to determine which paragraph (or sentence) you like least in the paper. Figure out why you don't like it, and work to make it better. Then go back through your paper and look for others like it.

Analyzing Your Work

If you've been considering the strengths and weaknesses of your paper, you've already begun to analyze your work. The process of analysis involves breaking down an idea or an argument into its parts and evaluating those parts on their merits. When you analyze your own paper, then, you're breaking down that paper into its parts and asking yourself whether or not these parts support the paper as you envision it.

The following checklist reiterates our earlier advice. Use it to analyze your whole paper, or use it to help you figure out what has gone wrong with a particular part of your work.

Consider your introduction:
> If you're writing a research paper, does the introduction place your argument in an ongoing conversation?
> If you're not writing a research paper, does the introduction establish context?
> Does the introduction define all of your key terms?
> Does the introduction draw the reader in?
> Does the introduction lead the reader clearly to your thesis?

Consider your thesis:

Does the thesis say what you want it to say?

Does the thesis make a point worth considering? Does it answer the question "So what?"

Does the thesis provide the reader with some sense of the paper's structure?

Does the paper deliver what your thesis promises to deliver?

Consider your structure:

Make an outline of the paper you've just written. Does this outline reflect your intentions?

Does this outline make sense, or are there gaps in the logic—places where you've asked your readers to make leaps for which they haven't been prepared?

Is each point in the outline adequately developed?

Is each point equally developed? (That is, does your paper seem balanced overall?)

Is each point relevant? Interesting?

Underline the thesis sentence and all of the topic sentences. Then cut and paste them together to form a paragraph. Does this paragraph make sense?

Consider your paragraphs:

Does each paragraph have a topic sentence that clearly controls it?

Are the paragraphs internally coherent?

Are the paragraphs externally coherent? (That is, have
you made adequate transitions between paragraphs? Is
each paragraph clearly related to the thesis?)

Consider your argument and its logic:

Have you really presented an argument, an assertion
worth making, or is your paper merely a series of
observations, a summary?

Do you see any holes in your argument, or do you find it
convincing?

Have you dealt fairly with the opposition, or have you
neglected to mention other possible arguments
concerning your topic for fear that they might under-
mine your own argument?

Have you supplied ample evidence for your arguments?

Consider your conclusion:

Does the conclusion sum up the main point of the paper?

Is the conclusion appropriate, or does it introduce a
completely new idea?

Does the language resonate, or does it fall flat?

Have you inflated the language in order to pad a conclusion that is empty and ineffective?

Does the conclusion leave the reader with something to
think about?

The final step that you'll want to take before submitting your
paper is to make sure that the grammar, spelling, and punc-

tuation throughout the paper are correct and that you've formatted it appropriately. These details may seem frustratingly minor, but errors often cause readers to grow impatient with otherwise well-written essays. So be sure to take the time to carefully proofread your essay.

When you proofread, you need to slow down your reading, allowing your eye to focus on every word, every phrase of your paper. Reading aloud is the most effective way to make yourself see and hear what you actually *wrote*, not just what you *meant*. Remember, a computer spellchecker is not an editor; for example, the word "form" will be spelled correctly, even if you meant "from." As you read, look for common errors—spelling errors, faulty subject-verb agreement, unclear pronoun antecedents, *its/it's* confusion, *their/there* confusion, and so on. If you have time, get the opinion of a second reader. Treat the proofreading stage as you would a word search or sudoku puzzle—that is, as a puzzle to be solved. No doubt, some errors are lurking in your prose (even professional writers find errors when they proofread their own work). Make it your mission to find them and root them out.

You'll also want to format the paper correctly. Some instructors provide explicit directions about constructing a title page, choosing a font, setting margins, paginating, footnoting, and so on. Be sure to follow these instructions carefully. If the instructor does not provide directions, consult the *MLA Handbook*—the standard reference for writers in the humanities—for specific advice. Instructors appreciate papers that are not only well written but also beautifully presented. In academic writing, "beauty" equals simplicity: no needless ornamentation, no fancy fonts, and nothing to distract the reader from the sound of your writer's voice and the clarity of your thoughts.